exhale

90 Devotions For Letting Go And Living In Unforced Rhythms Of Grace

90 Devotions For Letting Go And Living In Unforced Rhythms Of Grace

HOLLY NEWTON

Copyright © 2020 Holly Newton.

All rights reserved. No part of this book may be used or reproduced by any means, graphic, electronic, or mechanical, including photocopying, recording, taping or by any information storage retrieval system without the written permission of the author except in the case of brief quotations embodied in critical articles and reviews.

This book is a work of non-fiction. Unless otherwise noted, the author and the publisher make no explicit guarantees as to the accuracy of the information contained in this book and in some cases, names of people and places have been altered to protect their privacy.

WestBow Press books may be ordered through booksellers or by contacting:

WestBow Press
A Division of Thomas Nelson & Zondervan
1663 Liberty Drive
Bloomington, IN 47403
www.westbowpress.com
1 (866) 928-1240

Because of the dynamic nature of the Internet, any web addresses or links contained in this book may have changed since publication and may no longer be valid. The views expressed in this work are solely those of the author and do not necessarily reflect the views of the publisher, and the publisher hereby disclaims any responsibility for them.

Any people depicted in stock imagery provided by Getty Images are models, and such images are being used for illustrative purposes only.
Certain stock imagery © Getty Images.

Scripture quotations taken from The Holy Bible, New International Version® NIV® Copyright © 1973 1978 1984 2011 by Biblica, Inc. TM. Used by permission. All rights reserved worldwide.

ISBN: 978-1-6642-0432-4 (sc)
ISBN: 978-1-6642-0433-1 (hc)
ISBN: 978-1-6642-0431-7 (e)

Library of Congress Control Number: 2020917048

Print information available on the last page.

WestBow Press rev. date: 09/29/2020

*For Amos,
Your brief life on earth showed me more of
Jesus than I've known in a lifetime.*

In the pages of this devotional, you will find room to rest, receive, and renew as you journey through ninety days of seeking Jesus through His Word, learning to lean into His unforced rhythms of grace. I'm certain you will be encouraged as you discover for the first time or rediscover the truths about who God is and who He says you are.

Alex Seeley
Pastor of The BelongingCo & Author

In a fast-paced world, this is a must-read for anyone that is weary and seeking true rest. Holly allows us to slow down and go on a spiritual journey with her while rediscovering the truths about who God says we are. I can't recommend enough!

Rebekah Lyons
Bestselling Author, Rhythms of Renewal and You are Free

Holly has such a deep desire to see women live freely in the abundance and beauty that comes from knowing our Savior. In the inspiring pages of this devotional, you will find peace, purpose, and a renewed passion to seek Jesus through His Word. Holly writes from a place of knowing "the unexpected" well and provides the reader a roadmap to navigating the twists and turns of life with Jesus right by your side. Grab your Bible and a pen, and get ready to receive some solid Biblical truth while learning to walk confidently in victory!

Karen Harmon
Bettertogether.tv, Speaker, Writer, Business owner

I couldn't be more excited for Holly Newton's new devotional book, Exhale, to come out. Not only does Holly live this, but she shares her heart so beautifully. Through her down to earth writing style, her journey walking with God through mountain top seasons, and through deepest valleys, there are nuggets of wisdom and truth that our souls need.
I was a part of one of her beautiful Exhale Women retreats. My soul was refreshed! Find rest and find hope as you read these pages and EXHALE.

Jaime Jamgochian
Worship leader/Artist/Speaker/Songwriter/Author

Exhale comes at time when we all find ourselves collectively holding our breath ~ waiting for reprieve, for help and for hope. After experiencing the trauma of losing my husband at war I remember what a struggle it was to feel the Holy Spirit's breath and hear the voice of God through all the pain. This guided devotional would have been such a treasure for that season of trauma and trial. Whatever season you find yourself in, Exhale will meet you right where you're at and with exactly what you need for the day."

Ginger Ravella,
Co-Author Hope Found, USAF widow, Ambassador for the Gary Sinise Foundation

This devotional by my dear friend Holly is an invitation into intimacy with our Savior and a beckoning to redeeming the most inward places of your soul. Her personal journey with the Lord is reflected on these pages and has impacted so many lives including my own. I am certain you'll be encouraged, drawn in, and shaped into a more beautiful version of yourself, a closer reflection of who God intended you to be.

Tanya Hembree
Founder of ONYX + ALABASTER, Host of Black + White Sofa podcast

Contents

Preface xiii
How To Use This Devotional xv

Part 1: Created for Purpose: You Are Made For This 1

Part 1 Introduction 3
Day 1 5
Day 2 7
Day 3 9
Day 4 11
Day 5 13
Day 6 15
Day 8 18
Day 9 20
Day 10 22
Day 11 24
Day 12 26
Day 13 28
Day 15 31
Day 16 33
Day 17 35
Day 18 37
Day 19 39
Day 20 41
Day 22 44
Day 23 46
Day 24 48
Day 25 50
Day 26 52
Day 27 54
Day 29 57
Day 30 59

Part 2: Nothing To Prove: A Love Like This 61

Part 2 Introduction 63
Day 31 65

Day 32 67
Day 33 69
Day 34 71
Day 36 74
Day 37 76
Day 38 78
Day 39 80
Day 40 82
Day 41 84
Day 43 87
Day 44 89
Day 45 91
Day 46 93
Day 47 95
Day 48 97
Day 50 100
Day 51 102
Day 52 104
Day 53 106
Day 54 108
Day 55 110
Day 57 113
Day 58 115
Day 59 117
Day 60 119

Part 3: A Full Life In The Emptiest Places: Presence In The Pause 121

Part 3 Introduction 123
Day 61 125
Day 62 127
Day 64 130
Day 65 132
Day 66 134
Day 67 136
Day 68 138
Day 69 141
Day 71 144
Day 72 146

Day 73 148
Day 74 150
Day 75 152
Day 76 154
Day 78 157
Day 79 159
Day 80 161
Day 81 163
Day 82 165
Day 83 167
Day 85 170
Day 86 172
Day 87 174
Day 88 176
Day 89 178
Day 90 180

About the Author 213

Preface

More than anything, I want the words, thoughts, scriptures, and prayers in these pages to draw your heart closer to our Lord, our Savior, showing you how to let go of all that weighs you down and live in His unforced rhythms of grace. I've prayed this prayer for you every time I sat down to pour out on these pages.

God never meant for us to 'work for Him.' His story has always been to invite us into an intimate relationship to 'work with Him.' This idea was a paradigm shift for me several years ago. A moment I realized much of my life "burn out" and failures came from being exhausted, depleted, striving and living in my own strength; even doing all the right things, serving God – I wasn't letting Him into the deepest intimate parts of my soul.

Even our deepest desires realized can't compare with the soul-rest that comes from abiding in God and His presence. We long for something more than anything or anyone in this world can fulfill. Yet striving to achieve comes almost as naturally as breathing. God's Kingdom is the opposite. He created us for rhythms of grace and rest in His strength through the power of the Holy Spirit.

We want God's will for our lives, but when we try to work it out in our own strength, it becomes daunting. When our daily rhythms are dependent on what we can accomplish, we burn out; we give up, we doubt, we fear, we lose our identity.

This Devotional is for you if you've ever been:

Tired of doubting
Tired of comparing
Tired of striving
Tired of fear
Tired of being tired

In my personal journey, the Lord has shown me that it's in rest that we have room to receive revelation and healing. Rest isn't found in a vacation or holiday. It can be found every single day by intentionally shifting your thoughts, mind, and heart toward the Lord.

God has important work for us to do here on this earth, but we must do it in His strength and by the power of the Holy Spirit. There have been times in my life where I ran ahead with a plan instead of waiting on God's complete instructions. I have learned to wait on His timing. Activities, plans, information, and execution alone don't bring transformation; it's only God's presence and the power of the Holy Spirit that brings actual effectiveness with what God has purposed in our lives.

Are you tired? Worn out? Burned out on religion? Come to me. Getaway with me, and you'll recover your life. I'll show you how to take a real rest. Walk with me and work with me—watch how I do it. Learn the unforced rhythms of grace. I won't lay anything heavy or ill-fitting on you. Keep company with me, and you'll learn to live freely and lightly. Matthew 11:28-30, (MSG).

Jesus is inviting you to let go and live in His unforced rhythms of grace. Will you let go of your worries? In stillness and quietness, know He is the Lord, and He will show you which way to go, the next right thing to do, providing every step of the way.

How To Use This Devotional

Each daily reading has a section called *Linger*, and on every seventh day, there is a section called *Pause and Ponder*.

Linger is the space where you are invited to linger in God's word and presence as you seek Him in your story. I encourage you to write down your thoughts, prayers, and any scriptures and begin speaking them back to God. Our faith increases as we stand on His promises. When we speak the word of God, it causes real change in our lives.

Every *Linger* section includes four prompts:

Praise and Recall:
Praising God for who He is shifts our perspective and aligns our souls with Him. Recalling what He's done fuels our faith for today and the future.

    Yet a time is coming and has now come when the true worshipers will worship the Father in the Spirit and in truth, for they are the kind of worshipers the Father seeks. God is Spirit, and his worshipers must worship in the Spirit and in truth. John 4:23-24

Confess:
Confessing our sins frees us to be made right with God and to hear from Him.

    If we confess our sins, he is faithful and just and will forgive us our sins and purify us from all unrighteousness. 1 John 1:9

Ask:
God wants us to bring every desire, burden, thought, hope, dream, disappointment, request to Him.

    Do not be anxious about anything, but in every situation, by prayer and petition, with thanksgiving, present your requests to God. Philippians 4:6

Rest and Receive:
Jesus modeled how vital it is to find solitude to rest and hear from His Father.

    And the peace of God, which transcends all understanding, will guard your hearts and your minds in Christ Jesus. Philippians 4:7

Pause and Ponder is a section every seven days where you are invited to look across the previous week at your notes in *Linger* and take time to ponder all that God is speaking to you. The truths of God are worth taking time to let them sink deep.

I implore you to think of this Devotional as a guide, not a checklist. Your time with God is personal, and He desires to encounter you without limits. Prayer and action go hand in hand. Activity comes out of the relationship. Part of the reason Jesus wanted his disciples to go away with Him was to get some rest so that they would be strengthened by His grace to carry out His purpose for their lives. He wants the same for you.

Come with me by yourselves to a quiet place and get some rest. Mark 6:31

Part 1

Created for Purpose: You Are Made For This

Part 1 Introduction

God has a purpose and plan for your life to impact the world around you. The definition of purpose is: the reason for which something is done or created, or for which something exists.

God is the God of visions, dreams, deliverance, and provisions. He can resurrect something new out of debris in any area, no matter how impossible it may seem. It's elusive for anyone to think they have control over their lives. Throughout life, we will all face unexpected circumstances - good and hard. God gives us the grace, strength, and wisdom we need to get through things in life as they come.

As Believers, we can live from a place of victory when we face challenges and battles because God's promises are true. Days can be hard and hurt happens to all of us, but it doesn't have to own us.

Exodus 9:16 says, But I have raised you up for this very purpose, that I might show you my power and that my name might be proclaimed in all the earth.

Jesus came to give us life abundantly, and that doesn't mean waiting until Heaven to receive His promises. Too often, Christians lack knowledge or understanding that they can live in victory above the circumstances of life by accessing all that God has made available. Perhaps having misguided perceptions or, sadly, are content just to get by.

Jesus came so that we can not only overcome but also thrive in God's purposes and plans while we're on this earth. As long as He is God – and He will always be God - He can move in and through our lives in a way like never before.

Day 1

The Lord himself goes before you and will be with you; he will never leave you nor forsake you. Do not be afraid; do not be discouraged. The Lord is the one who goes ahead of you; He will be with you. He will not fail you or forsake you. Deuteronomy 31:8

In Deuteronomy 31, Moses commissions Joshua and prepares the Israelites for his departure. He summoned Joshua in the presence of all Israel beginning with, 'Be strong and courageous'. He knew fear and doubt had the potential to be a companion in the long unpredictable journey ahead. As complex as their situation seemed, God's promise was profoundly simple: He promised He would not fail or forsake them, and that He would always be with them.

Everything God does on earth comes through the life of a man or woman. Have you ever stopped to think about that?

> You are here on purpose with a purpose. Each of us has a vital role assigned by God and the way we live our lives is an expression of the revelation we have of God.

Revelation forms the expectation you have of God in your life. He has given us hundreds of promises and assurances that He will be with us, guide, provide, and never forsake us.

In God's mercy, He doesn't show us our life reel in one sitting. You have a stunning story of promise but there is a war. You have a very real enemy that has been strategizing and scheming against you since you were born – he has come to ruin all that God intended for your life. But that's not where the story ends. We are reborn into a perfect inheritance that can never perish, never be defiled, and never diminish.

Just as God prepared Joshua for the long unpredictable journey ahead that would ultimately take him to the promised land, He gives you promises and preparation for your promised land. You only need to receive and allow Him to do the work in and through you. Can you hear Him whispering today? 'Be strong and courageous. I am with you. I am for you.

In rest, trust and dependence we can walk lightly and live freely, fully.

Day 1 Linger

Praise and Recall

Confess

Ask

Rest and Receive

Day 2

He says, "Be still, and know that I am God; I will be exalted among the nations, I will be exalted in the earth. Psalm 46:10

If we could see our lives beginning to end, it would be overwhelming. Facing adversities, disappointments, and delays are inevitable. This is why God has given us so many promises and explicit instructions so that we can live in His strength, peace, and grace.

In this psalm, to be still means to stop striving, stop fighting, relax, to not be anxious. The Greek root of 'be still' means let go.

God plants seeds and dreams in our hearts. Nothing is truly solid, trustworthy, or lasting apart from or in God. The way God unfolds His plans for our lives is a process. It's not a sprint. It's a journey. Slowly through prayer and process, God-given dreams come to life, rising with blooms in places and seasons beyond our finite minds could imagine. For His glory, for our good.

Letting go, the stillness of soul and surrender is where we find freedom. Freedom to trust and let go of fears, doubt, and insecurities. Being still does not mean standstill. In the process, we keep moving forward as God directs and orders our steps, knowing He has the final victory.

Day 2 Linger

PRAISE AND RECALL

CONFESS

ASK

REST AND RECEIVE

Day 3

He determines the number of the stars and calls them each by name, Great is our Lord and mighty in power; his understanding has no limit. Psalm 147:4-5

The number of stars is still uncountable by science, yet God knows them by name. Have you ever doubted the nearness of God? Have you ever been troubled, lacking understanding of what was going on around you or in your life? We all have.

The dream and purposes of God for your life are significant. No matter if you feel Him near, no matter if you lack understanding, you can know He is near and is always working. The Word of God stands, no matter what outcome we may experience. In Matthew 6, Jesus speaks about seeking first the kingdom. He essentially says that things will work out, not necessarily according to our plans but to His.

When we place our attention and affection rightly on God, we find that He will always give us what we need. Even though it might not be what we want, He knows best. I've learned that nothing is added to my life by worrying about results and outcomes. Planning, thinking, processing. It's all futile unless it's in partnership with God. It's only in seeking Him that all good things are added to our lives according to His purpose.

The God of all graces will give you all the graces and provisions you need because He cares for you. He will confirm, strengthen, and establish you – for His glory and your good.

Day 3 Linger

Praise and Recall

_____
_____
_____
_____
_____

Confess

_____
_____
_____
_____
_____

Ask

_____
_____
_____
_____
_____

Rest and Receive

_____
_____
_____
_____

Day 4

Trust in the Lord with all your heart, and do not lean on your own understanding. In all your ways acknowledge him, and he will make straight your paths. Proverbs 3:5-6

Leaning means putting your whole weight into something, or we could say here, identifying your entire world with something - your full understanding. When we have important choices and decisions to make, it can be hard to trust the different voices, opinions. It can be hard to trust God – or even ourselves that we've heard from God.

But God knows what's best for us, and He can help us understand His voice. He is a better judge of what we want than even our fickle hearts are. We can trust God is leading us to a place of purpose because He created us.

Something about dying to this life and all of our expectations frees us. In every surrender, God gives us a more in-depth understanding of who He is, tearing down walls and limits we place on Him. He replaces our self-made boundaries with His courage to go to places we've never been.

Take some time where you're placing your trust. What can you learn from this scripture today?

Day 4 Linger

Praise and Recall

_____
_____
_____
_____
_____

Confess

_____
_____
_____
_____
_____

Ask

_____
_____
_____
_____
_____

Rest and Receive

_____
_____
_____
_____

Day 5

Many are the plans in a person's heart, but it is the Lord's purpose that prevails. Proverbs 19:21

Striving to achieve comes almost as naturally as breathing. When a goal grabs your attention, the human instinct is to "go for it" without thinking it through, investing time and energy. Later discovering it was the wrong pursuit.

Sometimes we want something so much that we work toward the goal without taking it to the Lord in prayer. He invites us to talk to Him before, during, and after a quest so that we can view it from His perspective. When we take the time to discuss matters and plans with Him, we experience peace and satisfaction. Be willing to discuss desires with Him in prayer. With confidence, know that what He places in your heart He will equip you to accomplish. God's plans exceed anything you could hope for or imagine.

Slow down today and ask God to help you focus on a specific area in your life that you have a tight grip on.

Is there an "I'll give you everything but_" area in your life? Is there an "I can probably handle_better than you can, God" are in your life?

If an area comes to mind, remember He already knows it and invites you to come just as you are.

Day 5 Linger

Praise and Recall

_____
_____
_____
_____
_____

Confess

_____
_____
_____
_____
_____

Ask

_____
_____
_____
_____
_____

Rest and Receive

_____
_____
_____
_____

Day 6

There is a time for everything and a season for every activity under the heavens. Ecclesiastes 3:1

He has made everything beautiful in it's time. He has also set eternity in the hearts of men; yet they cannot fathom what God has done from beginning to end. Ecclesiastes 3:11

What brings you joy, fulfillment, and satisfaction in life? Have you thought about it recently?

The phrase 'under the sun' occurs twenty-eight times in the book of Ecclesiastes. It describes a search for meaning and satisfaction that never moves beyond this life and world. It's a story of one person's anxious search for meaning. We read in Ecclesiastes that Solomon was a busy man and tried and did everything there was to do. But at the end of his experience, he was unfulfilled, exhausted, disappointed, and frustrated.

Earthly pursuits and pleasures will never wholly satisfy us because God has set eternity in the hearts of man. (Ecc. 3:11) We are created in His image and have a spiritual thirst for His presence and purposes. God has a plan for all people, and He has created cycles and seasons of life. The secret to peace in whatever pace you find yourself in today is trusting and appreciating God's perfect timing.

Seasons do change, and before every change, something is shifting in the unseen.

There is a work that occurs in the unseen that is necessary to new life. Everything hidden will eventually be revealed. It's a process.

God invites us into a relationship with Him, and He's so much more interested in our process than our destination on earth. He invites us into the hidden places to produce renewed hope as He reveals His love for us.

Day 6 Linger

PRAISE AND RECALL

___

CONFESS

___

ASK

___

REST AND RECEIVE

___

Day 7 Pause and Ponder

Day 8

But they that wait upon the Lord shall renew their strength; they shall mount up with wings as eagles; they shall run and not be weary; and they shall walk and not faint. Isaiah 40:31

Have you ever felt called by God, strongly, to pursue something? Beginning with bold excitement and courage, and then inevitably a bend in the road makes you question why it's so hard?

In wisdom and love, God gives us keys to renewal, hope, and vitality in scripture. When weariness sets in, the Holy Spirit can provide supernatural strength to endure and navigate the bends.

God never intended for us to live life in our finite strength. He gives us a promise of strength and power to help us rise above distractions and difficulties in life.

> He desires us to learn the rhythms of grace that breathe life into our spiritual walk to bring order and peace.

God is a promise-making and promise-keeping God, who has existed forever, created everything, including you. All power belongs to Him.

The narrative of our life is a reflection of what we believe about God. As you run your race today, where do you need the Lord to renew your strength?

Day 8 Linger

PRAISE AND RECALL

_____
_____
_____
_____
_____

CONFESS

_____
_____
_____
_____
_____

ASK

_____
_____
_____
_____
_____

REST AND RECEIVE

_____
_____
_____
_____

Day 9

I am doing something brand new, something unheard of. Even now, it sprouts and grows and matures. Don't you perceive it? I will make a way in the wilderness and open up flowing streams in the desert.
Isaiah 43:19

Have you ever hoped or prayed for God to do something unheard of?

> Dreaming is more than setting goals and a to-do list. It's partnering with God, who is limitless in bringing His purposes and plans alive in your life.

Sometimes we pray, and we don't get the answers we hope for. Sometimes we pray, and our plans get re-routed. Delay is a significant threat to our hope and faith if we don't fix our heart, soul, and mind on the faithfulness of God. God is not limited by time or circumstance.

Recalling what God has done reminds us of what He can do and fuels our faith. It's essential to know those past movements of God, and His miracles are nothing compared to what God can do in your future.

Day 9 Linger

PRAISE AND RECALL

_____
_____
_____
_____
_____

CONFESS

_____
_____
_____
_____
_____

ASK

_____
_____
_____
_____
_____

REST AND RECEIVE

_____
_____
_____

Day 10

Seek the Lord while he may be found; call on him while he is near.
Isaiah 55:6

What difference does Jesus make? He offers forgiveness, peace and reconciliation, and purpose and meaning. The Bible is one extended invitation to come to God. Jesus often invited people to come to Him. In Isaiah 55, God once again invites us to come.

The Bible is God's story. It holds the truth of the Kingdom of God, and the revelation of Jesus Christ. Whether aware or not, we are in this story.

It's the story of God, who created us in love, revealed Himself fully, and offers salvation through Jesus. By an outpouring of grace and mercy, He chooses to accomplish His purposes through us. It's a redemption story, and though God made way for our redemption story, it's His story all for His glory.

There's freedom in this. Do you see it? Freedom to not perform, to not strive, to not orchestrate on your own.

> Purposes and plans for your life are discovered in God. It's your job to abide and seek Him. It's His job to accomplish them.

To truly know God and live in His abundance of grace and joy and meaning, we must listen to Him speak. What is He saying to you today?

Day 10 Linger

PRAISE AND RECALL

CONFESS

ASK

REST AND RECEIVE

Day 11

For I know the plans I have for you," declares the Lord, "plans to prosper you and not to harm you, plans to give you hope and a future. Jeremiah 29:11

Are you sitting down? Is everything tidy and in order around you? Occasionally our circumstances seem to be exactly under control. I like to wait for those moments to start writing or work on the next project. I'm prone to spend an excessive amount of time setting my desk and the environment around me before I start an assignment. Most of the time though, for all of us, everything is not in complete order, and the excuses pile up to keep us from faithful obedience.

It's hard to lean in and flourish when you're waiting for everything to be perfect. In Jeremiah 29, we read that Judah was in exile, living in Babylon, with every reason to give up and let life grind to a halt. They had every right to hate the Babylonians. Still, Jeremiah instructed them to move ahead with their lives and to walk in ordinary daily obedience. He urged them to be a blessing to the nation they were in.

Here we learn much about the grace of God: obedience and blessings, repentance, and forgiveness. A leader who helps us move ahead, believes we can do the task, and who will be with us all the way is encouraging. That is our God. This is how He leads us. He knows the future, provides and goes with us as we fulfill His mission.

What are you doing with your time? What step of ordinary daily obedience can you take today? If you're not sure what to do next, simply ask Him. He wants to show you.

Day 11 Linger

PRAISE AND RECALL

_____
_____
_____
_____
_____

CONFESS

_____
_____
_____
_____
_____

ASK

_____
_____
_____
_____
_____

REST AND RECEIVE

_____
_____
_____
_____

Day 12

See, I am doing a new thing! Now it springs up; do you not perceive it? I am making a way in the wilderness and streams in the wasteland. Isaiah 43:19

Do you realize how valuable you are to God?

All of us will face trials and temptations. We'll go through 'the fire' and wade through 'rough waters.' Sometimes you cannot understand what's going on and will want to give up. But God often uses the challenges and difficulties of life to shape us. He uses them to strengthen your character and advance His purpose in your life.

God always acts in love (43:3-4). In all the struggles and difficulties, God has a good plan for your future. If you are in a 'desert' or 'wasteland' right now, trust God that He will make a way through.

> We'll never fully walk in our destiny if we are defining our future by our past.

The definition of new is: never existing before, brand new, up to the minute, current, advanced, newborn, fresh, original.

Past moves and miracles of God are nothing compared to what He can do in your future.

Day 12 Linger

Praise and Recall
_____
_____
_____
_____
_____

Confess
_____
_____
_____
_____
_____

Ask
_____
_____
_____
_____
_____

Rest and Receive
_____
_____
_____
_____

Day 13

Look at the nations and watch - and be utterly amazed. For I am going to do something in your days that you would not believe, even if you were told. Habakkuk 1:5

You have a stunning story of promise. God's desire in your life is to uncover and awaken the gifts and purposes He put within you. You don't have to understand your purpose and destiny all at once. You won't. God is more interested in our process than our destination. He wants us to come to Him with our struggles and doubts.

When Habakkuk cried out for answers in his time of struggle, God answered him with words of hope in Verse 5. We are so quick to define our identities by strengths and weaknesses, victories, and defeat. But God wants us to find our purpose and identity in who He says we are and the promises He's made.

Your purpose is not just about you. It's also about others. When you make life about loving God and others, seeking Him, and remaining surrendered, your purpose emerges. He has given us all different gifts to use for carrying out His purpose, and He gives us exactly what we need.

Is there any area you've believed lies about yourself? Find Scriptures to replace them and meditate on them for comfort and strength.

Day 13 Linger

Praise and Recall

___

Confess

___

Ask

___

Rest and Receive

___

Day 14 Pause and Ponder

Day 15

For the revelation awaits an appointed time; it speaks of the end and will not prove false. Though it linger, wait for it; it will certainly come and will not delay. Though the revelation lingers, wait for it; it will certainly come and will not delay. Habakkuk 2:3

In Habakkuk 2, we read God's response to Habbakuk's questions: How long would evil prevail? How long must I call for help? To God's people, it felt like a perpetual motion of law-keeping (Hab. 1:4). In their circumstance, they couldn't see any hope of the future God has promised them. They were waiting and pleading, imploring God to hear and save them.

God was also waiting, waiting for His perfect predetermined time. He's never worried about being too early or too late. He is present and works out plans in His perfect timing. Sometimes the waiting may feel punitive, but it's always in our best interest.

I imagine you're waiting for something today. I am waiting for things, too. We are all waiting for something. It can be tempting to believe we are the only ones waiting, and it can make us feel paralyzed. The longer the waiting, the greater temptation to think that God is ignorant of our prayers or holding out.

We don't have to understand the plans and purposes all at once. God wants to awaken our souls to His promises.

Bring Him your questions and emotions. He can handle it. He is also acting, right now, on your behalf. Your God will not fail.

Day 15 Linger

Praise and Recall

_____
_____
_____
_____
_____

Confess

_____
_____
_____
_____
_____

Ask

_____
_____
_____
_____
_____

Rest and Receive

_____
_____
_____
_____

Day 16

Are you tired? Worn out? Burned out on religion? Come to me. Get away with me and you'll recover your life. I'll show you how to take a real rest. Walk with me and work with me—watch how I do it. Learn the unforced rhythms of grace. I won't lay anything heavy or ill-fitting on you. Keep company with me and you'll learn to live freely and lightly. Matthew 11:28-30 (MSG)

Do you ever feel alone or like it's all up to you? Do you ever feel like peace is elusive? Blocked by layers of work you can't seem to get done. God's plan is different than the world's. The world says peace comes when you've achieved the goal, gained the approval of others, completed the job. It's exhausting just thinking about it.

Rest. Our souls crave it, don't they? We have to find spaces to be still, listen, and let go. While we can't take a break from what goes on in the world, we can learn to lean into the rhythms of God's grace. It's in rest that we gain revelation.

God calls us to stop working in our strength and cast our cares upon Him (1 Peter 5:7). In Matthew 11, Jesus is comparing our burdens to that of a yoke. A heavy wooden piece of equipment placed on oxen shoulders to work. He invites us to place all that is heavy and weighs us down on His shoulders - letting Him do the work.

It's not God's plan for you to run on empty. He walks among us, offering to remove that which bends our backs and breaks our hearts. He offers rest that seeps into the weariness of the soul. He provides us life-giving rhythms.

Do you need God's peace today in any area? It could be your mindset, health, family, friends, finance, anything that burdens you.

Offer that area of your life to God and meditate on what He's speaking. There's no haste in this place. Real rest knows no fear, no want, and is sure. To gain it, all we need to do is come.

Day 16 Linger

PRAISE AND RECALL
_____
_____
_____
_____
_____

CONFESS
_____
_____
_____
_____
_____

ASK
_____
_____
_____
_____
_____

REST AND RECEIVE
_____
_____
_____
_____

Day 17

But when he saw the wind, he was afraid and, beginning to sink, cried out, "Lord, save me! Matthew 14:30

In Matthew 14, we read the story of Peter climbing out of the boat and fighting through the wind and the waves as he began to walk on water. I think about the famous phrase "do it afraid" and how it characterizes Peter's action inspired by faith. He reacted to Jesus in faith, but on the water, fear replaced his faith, and it wasn't enough to sustain him.

The winds felt stronger out on the water than they did in the safety of the boat. The winds and Peter's fragility overtook him. Have you ever felt like that? It isn't the lack of ground that Peter feared the most. He began to experience the wind's powerful ability to sink him, and his confidence wavered. He put his focus on what the wind could do, taking his eyes off of what Jesus could do.

When Peter cried out for help as he was sinking, Jesus immediately reached out His hand and saved Him. He didn't accuse Peter. He invited him into a deeper connection and trust.

Are you living out of your comfort zone? Is there any area you need to refocus your faith in what God can do?

Day 17 Linger

Praise and Recall

Confess

Ask

Rest and Receive

Day 18

For whoever would save his life will lose it, but whoever loses his life for my sake will find it. Matthew 16:25

When we take time to listen to God, we will know His intentions for our lives. How do you hear the voice of God amid the noise and distractions of life?

We listen to God's voice through scriptures, through the words of Jesus, and in prayer. What Jesus spoke are the words of God. In every key decision we face, we must ask ourselves whether we have in mind the concerns of God or human concerns. What Jesus is saying to Peter in Matthew 16 is the heart of His mission, and it has enormous implications for all of His followers.

Seeking a life of comfort and security isn't what we're called to, though Jesus gives us protection. What Jesus said to His disciples applies to us as well. We're not in the driver's seat, and self-sacrifice is His way to finding your true self - this is the way to find life in its fullness. To gain anything else is to lose yourself.

If you follow Jesus and surrender your life to Him, you find the very purpose of life. God's purpose for our lives is far more fulfilling and important than seeking self-agenda.

Freedom to live God's purposes comes when we allow the presence of God into every area of our lives. Personal freedom is part of a larger picture of what God wants to do in us and through us. Because of Jesus, we don't have to live ordinary lives. It doesn't mean we don't have ordinary everyday moments. The difference is we have resurrection hope. He offers us strength and power to live in His authority. God wants to place His Holiness in our ordinary lives.

Day 18 Linger

Praise and Recall

_____
_____
_____
_____
_____

Confess

_____
_____
_____
_____
_____

Ask

_____
_____
_____
_____
_____

Rest and Receive

_____
_____
_____
_____

Day 19

To the Jews who had believed him, Jesus said, 'If you hold to my teaching, you are really my disciples. Then you will know the truth, and the truth will set you free. John 8:31-32

Do you want to live in true freedom to receive all that God has for your life?

Through Jesus, we can receive salvation and be set free from our sins. In John 8, Jesus is not only talking about salvation. He's also speaking about liberty. His work on the cross offers us freedom from sin and death. Living in liberty is a daily choice to choose His ways, power, and authority to align our actions and thoughts with that of the Kingdom. Jesus is our Savior, and He is our liberator.

Jesus' relationship with His Father was unique. But through Him, we can know God. The relationship between Jesus and His Father brings freedom to your life. Because through Jesus, the Son, we can be set free (v. 36).

Jesus is the narrow way, but He doesn't call us to be narrow-minded or anti-intellectual. Following Him is the way of intellectual freedom and integrity. Knowing Him increases your insight and widens your understanding.

Jesus is the truth. To live in a relationship with Him sets you free to be who God intended you to be, an original. He intended you to be an original, rather than a version of someone else.

Day 19 Linger

Praise and Recall

_____
_____
_____
_____
_____

Confess

_____
_____
_____
_____
_____

Ask

_____
_____
_____
_____
_____

Rest and Receive

_____
_____
_____
_____

Day 20

And we know that in all things God works for the good of those who love him, who have been called according to his purpose. Romans 8:28

You're meant to be a person of purpose. God promise in Romans 8:28 means He's at work on your behalf, shaping everything for your good. God will never leave you to figure it out on your own. He wants you to live from the truth that He has called you and build together with Him.

In life, it's easy to feel overwhelmed, overtired, or just plain over it. Setbacks and disappointment happen. But how we view God has a direct impact on how we handle delays. They aren't to harm us. God uses delays to prepare or protect us. It's the goodness of our God that wants to move us beyond discouragement to expectancy.

We don't have control over most circumstances of life, but we have the power of choice in how we respond. If we truly begin believing God is who He says He is and faithful to His promises, delay and disappointment can grow us rather than discourage us. The truth is, delays can become the set-up to the turn-around you've been hoping and praying for. It's a matter of perspective. You get to decide what truth is your foundation.

What did God put in you? What does His dream look like for your life? Do you need to rest and trust His promises in any area today?

Day 20 Linger

PRAISE AND RECALL

CONFESS

ASK

REST AND RECEIVE

Day 21 Pause and Ponder

Day 22

Do not conform to the pattern of this world, but be transformed by the renewing of your mind. Then you will be able to test and approve what God's will is—his good, pleasing, and perfect will. Romans 12:2

The world tells us that success, happiness, and freedom come from all of our desires being fulfilled. But I can say from experience ignoring spiritual disciplines only leads to chains, not freedom, and fulfillment. God does want to awaken the gifts and purposes He put within you. But there is no fast track to pursuing your God-given dreams.

Gaining God's perspective changes how we see ourselves, circumstances, purpose, and the world around us. Attending church, listening to that podcast is not the same as engaging with God. Only He can transform. Prayer, fasting, and Bible study are all disciplines that renew our minds and refresh our spirits. God is the giver of real spiritual growth that's formed in the Spirit's work within us. Not our efforts. As we surrender, we receive.

May our hearts be conformed to His likeness, quickened by His Spirit, and molded by His love.

Day 22 Linger

PRAISE AND RECALL

CONFESS

ASK

REST AND RECEIVE

Day 23

Be on your guard; stand firm in the faith; be courageous; be strong.
1 Corinthians 16:13

You are designed on purpose with love, intention, and care. The Gospel is the good news – an all-encompassing hope because of the life, death, and resurrection of Jesus Christ. It's real, and it's for right now.

God's dreams, purposes, and plans for your life are unique, and nobody can live it better than you. You were made for this. He knew we would face opposition because there is a real enemy to distract and destroy the plans God has for every person.

In today's scripture, Paul is writing to the Corinthians and urging them to be on their guard and be watchful for spiritual enemies that might slip in and sideline them. Whether it be divisions, sin, pride, disorder, he urged them to stand firm in what they believed – the Gospel they were taught at the beginning that brought them salvation. He told them to be firm with the strength of the Holy Spirit and do everything in love.

How do we stand firm against the war waged on our souls?

Think about a runner. I'm not one, but I've observed many. An experienced runner warms up, is equipped with appropriate clothing and shoes, uses proper form always looking up and ahead, aware of the course laid out in front of them.

To fully walk in God's calling, we must do the same – practice, be equipped, and run this race with eyes wide open and gazing forward. Think about it; if you run with eyes closed or looking backward, you will eventually hit a wall or even take a hard fall. God's word calls us to fix our eyes on Him – not temptation, circumstances, failures, fear.

Small daily frustrations can mount up and wear us down. No matter how your week is shaping up, know that God promises to be our source of power, courage, wisdom, and strength.

Day 23 Linger

Praise and Recall

_____
_____
_____
_____
_____

Confess

_____
_____
_____
_____
_____

Ask

_____
_____
_____
_____
_____

Rest and Receive

_____
_____
_____
_____

Day 24

So we do not lose heart. Though our outer self is wasting away, our inner self is being renewed day by day. For this light momentary affliction is preparing for us an eternal weight of glory beyond all comparison, as we look not to the things that are seen but to the things that are unseen. For the things that are seen are transient, but the things that are unseen are eternal. 2 Corinthians 4:16-18

We all have faced problems that have caused us to lose heart and want to think about quitting what we're doing – work, school – or a relationship. Rather than giving up, as Believers, we can draw on strength from the Holy Spirit. There's so much more than what you can see when you pray.

Your obedience and prayers are sowing seed for your future.

Because of Jesus, there is purpose in troubles and suffering. Your very weariness and weakness allow the resurrection power of Christ to strengthen you. There are benefits we gain in pain that reaches beyond our human limitations. They remind us of Jesus' suffering for us. They keep us humble and cause us to look beyond this brief life. Choosing faith when life is hard allows God to demonstrate His power in our lives.

This life is not all there is. Faith in Jesus is transformational, now and into eternity.

Day 24 Linger

PRAISE AND RECALL

_____
_____
_____
_____
_____

CONFESS

_____
_____
_____
_____
_____

ASK

_____
_____
_____
_____
_____

REST AND RECEIVE

_____
_____
_____
_____

Day 25

For we are God's handiwork, created in Christ Jesus to do good works, which God prepared in advance for us to do. Ephesians 2:10

The meaning of the word purpose is "why something is done or created or for which something exists or is done, made, used." God created us all with a purpose that He specifically designed just for us. It's unique and unequivocal to anyone else. Sometimes we settle for a life that is less-than-beautiful because we feel it's so far out of reach, or too difficult to achieve. We want so desperately to find it. What is purpose is all around us, and we simply need to stop resisting it? What if we're missing it because it doesn't look like we thought it would?

Are we listening to God, or are we searching for our place in this world with only our own needs in mind? So many voices in the world and things that pull for your attention. God created you with a purpose that will ultimately fulfill your soul. But it's only found in surrender to His will and hearing His voice.

There's so much life in letting go. Have you ever been in an endless season of stretching? In these moments, we're positioned for deeper revelations of God. Sometimes we have to let go of what we think is best to receive His best in a new season.

Following God is a risky thing – not because He changes. He doesn't. He is faithful and keeps His Promises. The risk is when you follow after God and begin to walk in His purposes, there will be earthly losses and gains, acceptance, and rejection. He never said it would be easy. He said we have to pick up our cross and follow Him. Jesus's Cross was His purpose and He calls us to pick up our cross (our purpose) daily and follow Him.

Is there something God is nudging you to let go of? I've learned that He never asks us to let go of something to keep us from our purpose, our calling. He asks us to let go to make room for all that He has planned for our lives. I promise, friend - you can trust Him.

Take time today to reflect on whom or what are you listening to and realign with God's voice if you need to.

Day 25 Linger

PRAISE AND RECALL
_____
_____
_____
_____
_____

CONFESS
_____
_____
_____
_____
_____

ASK
_____
_____
_____
_____
_____

REST AND RECEIVE
_____
_____
_____
_____

Day 26

Finally, brothers and sisters, whatever is true, whatever is noble, whatever is right, whatever is pure, whatever is lovely, whatever is admirable–if anything is excellent or praiseworthy–think about such things. Philippians 4:8

Just like our bodies reflect what we eat, our heart and soul reveal what we think on and what we take in with our eyes and ears. God's peace is not like the world's peace. Positive thinking or absence of conflict don't bring peace. It comes from confidence, knowing God is in control.

Guarding our hearts is imperative. What goes in our minds determines what comes out in our words and actions. God created us spirit, soul, and body (1 Thes. 5), and we must care for every part of how He created us so we can live out His plans the way He created us to live.

We find soul satisfaction in God's wisdom and peace. Worry can wreak havoc on our lives. Some of our fears are real, but some are illusionary. In either case, a life weighed down by worry isn't really living. In Philippians 4, Paul urges us to pray every time a concern enters our minds, and give God thanks.

Praise shifts our focus from troubles to possibilities.

In the Bible, peace means completeness, fulfillment, wholeness, harmony, security, and well being. We are surrounded by messages daily that can easily tempt us with wrong thoughts. The best way to position yourself for right thinking is to occupy your mind with whatever is true, noble, right, pure, lovely, admirable, and praiseworthy (Phil. 4:8).

Take time today to write down specific requests and needs in your life. Then take time to give thanks to God not only for what He has done but for what He will do.

Day 26 Linger

PRAISE AND RECALL

___

CONFESS

___

ASK

___

REST AND RECEIVE

___

Day 27

Therefore since we are surrounded by such a great cloud of witnesses, let us throw off everything that hinders and the sin that so easily entangles. And let us run with perseverance the race marked out for us, fixing our eyes on Jesus, the pioneer, and perfecter of faith. For the joy set before him, he endured the cross, scorning its shame, and sat down at the right hand of the throne of God. Hebrews 12:1-2

The writer of Hebrews compares life to running a race. It's more of a marathon than a sprint, and it requires endurance and discipline. There is a race marked for you that you are urged to run with perseverance.

Difficulties, opposition, wrong choices, and challenges can trip you up along the way. The key to endurance is keeping your eyes fixed on Jesus. It puts life in perspective. Running a good race requires training. It's hard work, and sometimes training is painful heart work. But it's worth it. Nothing great is accomplished without endurance and perseverance.

Sometimes we have to lose and let go to learn to persevere so we can receive all that God has for our lives.

> Perseverance is choosing faith to trust again when you've experienced loss, disappointment, and hurt.

It's choosing to throw off fear, discouragement, doubt. It takes intentional preparation.

Jesus knew there was a great joy on the other side of the suffering He would endure on the cross. Remember, you do not struggle alone. Because Jesus already won, our final victory will be so sweet.

Day 27 Linger

PRAISE AND RECALL

_____
_____
_____
_____
_____

CONFESS

_____
_____
_____
_____
_____

ASK

_____
_____
_____
_____
_____

REST AND RECEIVE

_____
_____
_____

Day 28 Pause and Ponder

Day 29

But the wisdom that comes from heaven is first of all pure; then peace-loving, considerate, submissive, full of mercy and good fruit, impartial and sincere. Peacemakers who sow in peace raise a harvest of righteousness. James 3:17-18

Where we choose to turn for wisdom dramatically affects the course of our journey. We need to be careful whom we trust to speak into our lives. The Lord speaks through people, but we must weigh the words of others with the help of the Holy Spirit to discern what God is saying. Ultimately we need His wisdom; wisdom from Heaven.

Read James 3:13-18. Here we read James describing two kinds of wisdom. He describes bitter envy and selfish ambition in the heart of man as earthly and unspiritual – going so far as calling it demonic.

There is a sharp distinction between earthly and Heavenly wisdom. James goes on to describe what godly "wisdom from above" looks like. Wisdom from God is pure, peace-loving, considerate, full of mercy, and good fruits (v. 17). The life of Jesus and His words are our ultimate example of godly wisdom.

Is there any area you need wisdom today? Your Heavenly Father longs to be gracious to you and generously gives wisdom when asked (James 1:5). You'll know it's His wisdom. It carries gentleness and peace.

Day 29 Linger

Praise and Recall

Confess

Ask

Rest and Receive

Day 30

Humble yourselves, therefore under God's mighty hand, that he may lift you up in due time. Cast all your anxiety on him because he cares for you. 1 Peter 5:6-7

Tucked in 1 Peter 5, Peter interrupts his writings on suffering and Christian living in an ungodly culture in order to talk to church leadership, giving them an admonition to serve the people of God well. He knew that wise counsel and tender care would be critical in helping God's people persevere.

Humility is a mark of a wise and mature Christian. Peter advises us to remember that it's God's recognition that counts. Worrying about position or status is futile. God is able and willing to bless our lives in His perfect timing.

Humility is not thinking less of yourself; it's thinking of yourself less and thinking of others more. We put on humility when we choose to believe the best about someone, when we extend grace, when we focus on our leaders' strengths, when we gladly serve. Could it be that humility makes us more comfortable in less than ideal circumstances and even conflict?

Could this charge to be clothed in humility help you stretch in grace, endure with patience, or extend forgiveness?

Day 30 Linger

Part 2

Nothing To Prove:
A Love Like This

Part 2 Introduction

Matthew 11 opens with Jesus teaching about the kingdom and John in prison. As John sat in prison, he began to have doubts if Jesus was the Messiah. And he doubted his own purpose to prepare people for the coming Messiah. He questioned why he was sitting in prison when he could have been preaching to the crowds and preparing their hearts to see Jesus. His circumstances certainly didn't match up to what he knew his purpose was.

John sent his disciples to ask Jesus if he was who He said He was.

Jesus answered John's doubts by pointing to the acts of healing the blind, lame, deaf, curing lepers, raising dead, preaching the good news to the poor. With so much evidence, Jesus' identity was obvious.

Have you ever felt like John? Have you ever doubted God's work in your life because your current circumstances didn't match up to what you thought God wants for your life? John did. I think it's safe to say we all have at some point.

Doubt can tempt us to distance ourselves from God. But He says come closer, and we'll actually be blessed when we do. Matthew 11:6 says, Blessed is the man who does not fall away on account of me.

Jesus not only pointed to miracles to prove who He was, but He also turned to the crowd and confirmed John's identity. He confirmed who John was and his purpose, to others. We don't have to prove ourselves to others.

In Matthew 11:16-17, we read that Jesus condemned the attitude of his generation. No matter what He said or did, they took the opposite view. They were cynical and skeptical because He challenged their comfortable, secure, and self-centered lives.

Hearing God may require us to change the way we live, our perspective.

Are you wise in your own eyes? Or do you seek truth in childlike faith? Matthew 11:25

No one knows the Father except the Son and those to whom the Son chooses to reveal him. Matthew 11:27

Revelations of God are found when we seek Him with childlike faith. To "know" God means more than knowledge. Knowing God comes from an intimate relationship with Him.

John doubted his purpose.

Jesus confirmed his identity.

We don't have to strive to prove ourselves. We only need to walk in an intimate relationship with Jesus.

Are you carrying sin, excessive demands, oppression or persecution, or weariness in the search for God? Jesus wants to free you from these burdens. The rest that Jesus promises is love, healing, and peace with God. Not the end of all labor. He changes meaningless, wearisome toil into spiritual productivity and purpose.

Day 31

The Lord foils the plans of the nations; he thwarts the purposes of the peoples. But the plans of the Lord stand firm forever, the purposes of his heart through all generations. Psalm 33:10-11

What does the future hold? There are many things about the future that we don't know and that we're not supposed to know. However, there are other things that you can know about the future, and that makes a real difference in your life now. The scriptures tell us that the plans of the Lord stand and that He is faithful.

In Psalm 33:1-11, the author is reflecting on what God has done and His faithfulness. It's important to remember what God has done in the past because it gives us confidence for what He can do in our future.

God is the one who is the source of all that is right and true. He is faithful and loves righteousness and justice; (v. 4-5). Ultimately, He is in control of history, and the future for your life.

Putting your trust and hope in earthly power, knowledge, social connections, and the ability to plan is useless. The Christian life is a battle. It holds obstacles, challenges, blessings, victories. The nature of every trial varies. The struggles we face are a triple threat: the world, our flesh, and the enemy.

But with God, we can navigate the spiritual battles of life and rise above in His power.

> The key to winning is not to rely on your strength or opinions of others, but to put your trust in God.

This is so opposite of our culture, but at the end of the day, human strength and power will never be enough.

Is there an area you've slipped into relying on your strength? God wants to equip you with His.

Day 31 Linger

PRAISE AND RECALL

_____
_____
_____
_____
_____

CONFESS

_____
_____
_____
_____
_____

ASK

_____
_____
_____
_____
_____

REST AND RECEIVE

_____
_____
_____
_____

Day 32

The life that pleases me is a life lived in the gratitude of grace, always choosing to walk with me in what is right. This is the sacrifice I desire from you. If you do this, more of my salvation will unfold for you. Psalm 50:23 (TPT)

Can thankfulness change your day? Our day to day challenges can pull us under. When we allow the troubles of our days to control our perspective, we miss out on the possibilities. But what if we let the promises of God and gratitude help us rise above?

Why is it important to give thanks?

When we give thanks to God and praise Him, we are reminding ourselves of who He is. It takes our eyes off of what we can see so that we can believe Him for what we don't see yet.

We read in Luke 17 that Jesus healed all ten lepers, but only one returned to thank Him. It's possible to receive God's great gifts with an ungrateful spirit – nine of the ten men did so. Only the thankful man learned that his faith had played a role in his healing. When we are grateful, we grow in understanding of God's grace. God never demands that we thank him, but He is so pleased when we do, and He uses our responsiveness to teach us more about Himself.

Not only was this man a leper, but he was also a Samaritan – a race despised by the Jews. Luke is pointing out here that God's grace is for everyone. In Luke 17, Jesus said to the leper who returned to thank Him that his faith saved him (YLT). In Greek, the word saved means Sozo. Sozo means salvation – true wellness, complete wholeness. To live in sozo is to live life to the full. Jesus came so we can do this. He healed the leper, and what's more, He came to heal our leprosy – our sin, our disease.

Day 32 Linger

PRAISE AND RECALL

CONFESS

ASK

REST AND RECEIVE

Day 33

For as high as the heavens are above the earth, so great is his love for those who fear him; as far as the east is from the west, so far has he removed our transgressions from us. As a father has compassion on his children, so the Lord has compassion on those who fear him; for he knows how we are formed, he remembers that we are dust.
Psalm 103:11-14

God's love is long-suffering, compassionate with grace and mercy, especially toward His people.

We were made for God's love. We tend to compare God's love to what we experience through other imperfect people, who like ourselves love imperfectly. Yet God knows us and still chooses to reveal Himself and make His ways known to us. The Bible is full of scripture that implores us to see love from Heaven's perspective, not our own broken experiences.

Everything God did and does is loving. The greatest act of love, sending His Son to earth to live, die on the cross, and raising Him conquering death so we can one day be with our Father for eternity. Because of this love, we can receive the Lord's compassion and forgiveness. We can live in freedom.

This is the love of God.

Is there any area you need a deeper grasp of His love today? Take time to read meditate on Psalm 103 as you linger today. His love is everlasting.

Day 33 Linger

PRAISE AND RECALL

_____
_____
_____
_____
_____

CONFESS

_____
_____
_____
_____
_____

ASK

_____
_____
_____
_____
_____

REST AND RECEIVE

_____
_____
_____
_____

Day 34

Let love and faithfulness never leave you; bind them around your neck, write them on the tablet of your heart. Then you will win favor and a good name in the sight of God and man. Proverbs 3:3-4

Love and faithfulness are important character qualities. The Lord gives us teachings and commands to preserve and prosper us. 1 Corinthians 13:1 tells us that if we do everything according to His commandments but don't have love, we are nothing. That's an emphatic insight on how important it is to God that we know His love and that we live His love.

Love and loyalty should be deeply embedded in our hearts and be our guiding principles. Not the way the world loves, but the way God loves and has shown us how to love. Loyalty is being trustworthy and honoring others. It's saying and doing truth.

What does it mean to bind them around your neck? God wants us to remember these virtues when we wake when we go throughout our day. In every circumstance, in every relationship. This is looking at love and truth through wisdom. It's how God's world works.

What does it mean for love and faithfulness to be written on the tablet of your heart? It means to let them go deep so that you live them genuinely from the inside out. The outcome of loving faithfulness is God's favor, others' respect, and good relationships. Who wouldn't want that?

What's one way you can put these verses into action today?

Day 34 Linger

PRAISE AND RECALL

CONFESS

ASK

REST AND RECEIVE

Day 35 Pause and Ponder

Day 36

Forget the former things; do not dwell on the past. See, I am doing a new thing! Now it springs up; do you not perceive it? I am making a way in the wilderness and streams in the wasteland. Isaiah 43:18-19

God's love and plans for us are expansive, beyond our limited knowledge and understanding. Our lives are so important to Him. His love for each one of us reaches far before our lives began.

There are seasons in every life when you have to let go of your definition of what defines you to move towards all that God has for you entirely.

As I reflect on problems, delays, interruptions, and the unexpected I've encountered across the years, I can truthfully say I see the hand of God moving sovereign in my life. Long before there ever was a problem, there was a promise—a promise of God who loves deeper and higher than we can understand this side of Heaven.

Sometimes we can't see the new thing God wants to do in our life. We limit Him because we can't let go of comfort and familiarity. Or, we can't let go of our idea of how life should play out, what we should be doing when all along God has a grand plan to unfold across seasons and process.

> Holding tight to your comfort and limited understanding is a big thief of courage for your future. Ultimately, it can rob you of your destiny.

Let's not miss God at work. Our past has brought us to our present, but it doesn't determine our future. Whatever you have experienced, no matter how great or hard, it's nothing compared to what God can do.

The heart work is worth it. Is there any area you are limiting God? Are you stuck in comfort and familiarity? Talk to Him about it today.

Day 36 Linger

PRAISE AND RECALL

___

CONFESS

___

ASK

___

REST AND RECEIVE

Day 37

Enlarge the place of your tent, stretch your tent curtains wide, do not hold back; lengthen your cords, strengthen your stakes. Isaiah 54:2

God has given us a heritage. In Isaiah 54, God is speaking a future and hope over a childless woman, promising her she would not suffer shame and that she would have many descendants. Here in verse 2, He is giving her instructions on how to prepare to receive the blessing. He's calling her to action.

In God's great love and care for us, many times before we can see hope or promise fulfilled, He is making a way behind the scenes according to His purposes. And He calls us to an act of obedience before the blessing. He calls us to posture our lives and hearts to receive. Before we can ever walk in all that God has for us, we must prepare, expect, pray, and believe.

> The world tells us every day who we are not. God tells us who we are.

What if you positioned yourself today to let Him come through on your behalf? Laying down fear and striving, in faith-filled expectancy.

Day 37 Linger

PRAISE AND RECALL

CONFESS

ASK

REST AND RECEIVE

Day 38

No weapon forged against you will prevail, and you will refute every tongue that accuses you. This is the heritage of the servants of the Lord, and this is their vindication from me," declares the Lord.
Isaiah 54:17

It's impossible to overstate our need for a Savior and the love of Christ. Repentance and restoration is the message of Isaiah, illustrating the salvation we so desperately need, and the salvation given us in the completed work of Jesus Christ.

Have you ever felt under siege? Perhaps from circumstances that were a result of opposition from others or personal failure. The good news is Jesus loves you so much that He died instead of you. He took the punishment of the cross so we can be made whole. Jesus knew what it was like to be under siege, to sweat drops of blood. His love for us is so great; He made a choice to suffer so that we can live and so we can be free.

The desire to live in freedom and flourish is deep within every living thing and every created being. You're an original created by God, and your life was not meant to look like anyone else's.

Culture and social media frequently send counter messages to the truths and love of God.

> When we allow His truth to drown out the noise, it preserves our souls and prepares us for His purposes.

There is an original God-created destiny for your life. So, be you. Out of billions on the earth, this world needs you to who God created you to be - and He made you to flourish.

Peace, righteousness, security, and triumph over opposition belong to those who belong to God.

Day 38 Linger

PRAISE AND RECALL

_____
_____
_____
_____
_____

CONFESS

_____
_____
_____
_____
_____

ASK

_____
_____
_____
_____
_____

REST AND RECEIVE

_____
_____
_____
_____

Day 39

Call to me, and I will answer you, and show you great and mighty things which you do not know. Jeremiah 33:3

Have you ever considered how important it is to say thank you to God and to praise Him?

Worship positions our minds for renewal and our ears to hear from God. When we pray from a posture of gratitude - thanking God for what He's already done and for what He will do next - we magnify the power and sovereignty of God over our problems.

It's so easy to get caught up in our concerns that we don't slow down enough to say "thank you" to God when He answers our prayers. Have you ever been so excited to receive an answer to prayer that you forgot to mention thank you? I have. When that happens, and I become aware, I instantly repent and praise Him.

God doesn't want to control us, and He won't. Gratitude and praise shift our souls and vision to come in line with the Kingdom because we are made to worship.

I love how The Message version says in Philippians 4:6-7, that praises shape worries into prayers and in that God's wholeness will settle us down. God's peace is different from the world's peace. Positive thinking does not bring true peace. It comes from knowing that God is in control.

> Giving thanks to God helps unlock what He has for us and helps us to see from His perspective.

Sometimes it is a sacrifice to give praise and thanks. But when we choose a heart of thanksgiving, God doesn't just work to shift our situations, He changes our hearts, and we're strengthened. There is so much waiting for you on the other side of giving thanks. The effectiveness of how we pray is often based on the place we pray from.

Read Jeremiah 33. Take some time today to pause, pray, and give thanks. God has a solution for every problem you will ever encounter, and He longs to reveal His heart to you.

Day 39 Linger

PRAISE AND RECALL

_____
_____
_____
_____
_____

CONFESS

_____
_____
_____
_____
_____

ASK

_____
_____
_____
_____
_____

REST AND RECEIVE

_____
_____
_____
_____

Day 40

Not only that, but we rejoice in our sufferings, knowing that suffering produces endurance, and endurance produces character, and character produces hope, and hope does not put us to shame, because God's love has been poured into our hearts through the Holy Spirit who has been given to us. Romans 5:3-3 (ESV)

When we're at a loss for words, God's words have the power to change our thinking, our hearts, and circumstances. We have a reason to hope! His name is Jesus. As Believers, we can live hopeful no matter what is going on around us. Prayer, praise, and hope is never a waste of time.

When we face obstacles, God wants to bring breakthroughs and advancement in our lives. For His glory - and our good. He's the God of solutions, regardless of the problem.

We're in a unique time in our world facing unprecedented struggles. Instead of retreating in fear, let's lean in, abide, pray, praise, and declare all of God's promises. This is the most likely season for miracles and breakthroughs because God has already conquered every impossibility.

Isaiah 40:4-5 says, Every valley shall be raised up, every mountain and hill made low; the rough ground shall become level, the rugged places a plain. And the glory of the Lord will be revealed. And all mankind together will see it. For the mouth of the Lord has spoken.

In seasons of adversity, we need to be awake for what the Lord is doing. The rough ground is a picture of life's trials. We are not immune to them, but they never need to shake us - because our God is unshakeable.

In trials and sufferings, prepare to see God's work. Remove all obstacles and watch Him move. I have seen God move suddenly; in darkest hours. And, I have experienced the ultimate miracle of healing and breakthroughs. In every circumstance and situation, the miracle has always been and will always be Jesus.

Day 40 Linger

PRAISE AND RECALL

CONFESS

ASK

REST AND RECEIVE

Day 41

If I speak in the tongues of men or of angels, but do not have love, I am only a resounding gong or a clanging cymbal. If I have the gift of prophecy and can fathom all mysteries and all knowledge, and if I have a faith that can move mountains, but do not have love, I am nothing. If I give all I possess to the poor and give over my body to hardship that I may boast, but do not have love, I gain nothing.
1 Corinthians 13:1-3

Are we full of good intentions – but empty of love? Are we known by what we do or how we love?

In 1 Corinthians Chapter 12, Paul speaks of the gifts of the Spirit. Here in 1 Corinthians Chapter 13 we come to the fruits of the Spirit. We read Paul hinting that the fruits of the Spirit are more important than the gifts of the Spirit. Becoming loving people is far more important than whether we are busy, active people. Both are necessary, but one is greater.

In Galatians 5 Paul tells us that the fruit of the Spirit is love, joy, peace, patience, kindness, goodness, faithfulness, gentleness, and self-control – all manifestations of love. Once you have love, all of these other qualities are possible for you.

In 1 Corinthians 13, Paul is talking about agape love, a commitment of the will to uphold and cherish another person. Agape love describes the love of God. It's a word addressed to the will. It's a decision that you make and a commitment to treat another person with concern, care, and thoughtfulness, and to work for his or her best interests. To love like this, first, we have to love God. Any other attempt is in our own strength, a fleshly kind of love.

When you become aware of how God has loved you and how He loves you, love for Him isn't difficult. When you love God, you awaken your capacity to love people. Love is a supernatural quality that only comes from God alone.

What does today's reading infer about our intimacy with God, who is Love?

Day 41 Linger

PRAISE AND RECALL
___

CONFESS
___

ASK
___

REST AND RECEIVE
___

Day 42 Pause and Ponder

Day 43

Love is patient, love is kind. It does not envy, it does not boast, it is not proud. It does not dishonor others, it is not self-seeking, it is not easily angered, it keeps no record of wrongs. Love does not delight in evil but rejoices with the truth. 1 Corinthians 13:4-6

What keeps us from being patient with people?

Love is really only three simple things. In today's verse, we read that love is three positive things; all the rest are negatives. Love is patient, kind, and honest (rejoices in the truth). The negatives given here are things we must set aside to let the love of God manifest itself through our lives and our purpose. When we get the things that are hindering love out of the way, we can let the love of God flow through us. It's dying to self – this is the cross and the way to love. God is ready to love through us.

Patience and kindness. What are the things that stop that?

First on Paul's list is jealousy. If we don't love as God does, we can quickly become spiteful and short with people when we see them have something we want. It could be a quality, a relationship, position (you fill in the blank).

Next on Paul's list is boastful. Often we aren't patient because we have areas of pride. We like to brag about ourselves and seek the approval of others. But that must be surrendered for agape love to exist.

Then Paul says, love is not self-seeking, arrogant. Arrogance is disdain or lack of respect for another person. Love isn't dishonoring and rude. This is to ignore another's rights, to be haughty or sarcastic. Love puts others above oneself. It doesn't insist on it's own way. It's not stubborn and inflexible. Love is not irritable or resentful. Nothing destroys human relationships more than that.

Finally, love is not gloating over other people's troubles. It is secure. And when we have the love of God in us, we are able to live secure, confident, lives allowing the agape love of God to work in us and through us.

Day 43 Linger

PRAISE AND RECALL

_____
_____
_____
_____
_____

CONFESS

_____
_____
_____
_____
_____

ASK

_____
_____
_____
_____
_____

REST AND RECEIVE

_____
_____
_____
_____

Day 44

It always protects, always trusts, always hopes, always perseveres.
1 Corinthians 13:7

Love covers everything. It literally means to protect. It doesn't delight to expose the weaknesses of others.

Loves trusts. It doesn't mean to be gullible. It gives second chances, ready to trust anew.

Love hopes. There is no person or situation that is hopeless. There is always a place to begin again.

Love perseveres. It never quits and never gives up on anyone.

The love of Jesus protects, covers, gives new chances over and again, hopes, never quits, and never gives up on you – on anyone. This is the love the Holy Spirit wants to reproduce in us, so we are always becoming more loving.

Lord, help us to let your love be manifested in our lives, in our families, in our homes, and to every person in every place you lead us to.

Day 44 Linger

Praise and Recall

Confess

Ask

Rest and Receive

Day 45

Love never fails. But where there are prophecies, they will cease; where there are tongues, they will be stilled: where there is knowledge, it will pass away. For we know in part and we prophesy in part, but when perfection comes, the imperfect disappears. 1 Corinthians 13:8-10

What is this perfect thing which gradually increases in our lives, replacing our concerns about gifts?

If we take 1 Corinthians in full context and what has been said in surrounding passages, it's clear that the word "perfect" refers to love. Love is the perfect thing, which as it grows in our lives, it replaces all concern with the gifts we receive. We find ourselves growing into the revelation that the gifts the Spirit gives us are designed to lead us, rather than a means to an end.

Love is more important than all the spiritual gifts exercised in the Church. Love makes our actions and gifts useful.

Take a moment to reflect today and examine if there's an area where you've put the gifts of the Spirit above true, agape Love.

Day 45 Linger

PRAISE AND RECALL

CONFESS

ASK

REST AND RECEIVE

Day 46

When I was a child, I talked like a child, I thought like a child, I reasoned like a child. When I became a man, I put childish ways behind me. Now we see but a poor reflection as in a mirror; then we shall see face to face. Now I know in part; then I shall know fully, even as I am fully known. 1 Corinthians 13:11-12

God fully knows you and fully loves you. His love is so extravagant. Long before you drew your first breath, He was thinking about you. His love is not a love you have to earn. You only need to receive it. It's real, and He invites you to come as you are.

Some days we feel lovable, and some days we feel less than lovely. God's love is extravagant and never ceasing. No matter how you feel today, God wants you just to come as you are to Him. The one great we need we have is love, more love for God, and toward one another.

The ancient mirrors Paul refers to in today's verse are not mirrors like we have today. They were a high polished metal that only reflected a blurry image. Paul compares this blurriness of our perceptions today to the clarity we will have when we see Jesus face to face.

Your closest moments with the Lord are nothing compared to what you will experience when you find yourself face to face with Him and His holiness. Every concern will fade. In the very presence of God, you will be made perfect and complete.

As you spend time with God and go through your day today remember you carry the hope of Heaven.

Day 46 Linger

PRAISE AND RECALL

___

CONFESS

___

ASK

___

REST AND RECEIVE

___

Day 47

And now these three remain: faith, hope and love. But the greatest of these is love. 1 Corinthians 13:13

One day all of our questions will be answered, and all of our problems resolved when we see Jesus face to face. Faith is a simple, deliberate response to the provision of God. It will remain because we will go on responding to God throughout eternity. Hope is the expectation of yet more to come. God will continue to show us deeper revelations, ever-increasing because He is infinite. Love will remain too. The reason love is the greatest of faith, hope, and love is that God is Love.

To learn to love is to become more like God. It's the paramount value of life now and eternal life to come. It's what it's all about, isn't it?

The lie that Adam and Eve believed in the Garden of Eden was that if they disobeyed God, they would become like God and have a fulfilled life; that in obeying God, they would live a life less fulfilling. That lie, and its devastating results are still visible in the world around us today. The Word of God says to trust Him, follow Him, and love like Him.

When we see God, we will be like Him, for we will see Him as He is (1 John 3:2). Therefore, love remains.

Lord, help us to make love our goal, beginning today, next week, and the rest of our lives.

Day 47 Linger

PRAISE AND RECALL

CONFESS

ASK

REST AND RECEIVE

Day 48

Therefore we do not lose heart. Though outwardly we are wasting away, yet inwardly we are being renewed day by day. For our light and momentary troubles are achieving for us an eternal glory that far outweighs them all. So we fix our eyes not on what is seen, but on what is unseen, since what is seen is temporary, but what is unseen is eternal. 2 Corinthians 4:16-18

Whether we realize it or not, everything within us cries out for eternity (Ecc. 3:11). And everything in scripture points to it. God's work with us is not finished in this life. Life has its pressures and problems, but there is so much more for us to experience beyond time. Something so vast that only eternity is big enough to contain it.

Struggles, delays, disappointments – all that we go through are only preparing us for something yet to come. Day by day, we have to renew our minds and set our hearts on the faithfulness of God. If we don't, we'll burn out and give up. God's plans for our lives have intentional timing and rhythm.

What you do here on earth matters, but it doesn't end here. Our present experience is not purposeless and futile. There are purposes that carry eternal weight within you.

Day 48 Linger

PRAISE AND RECALL

CONFESS

ASK

REST AND RECEIVE

Day 49 Pause and Ponder

Day 50

It is for freedom that Christ has set us free. Stand firm, then, and do not let yourselves be burdened by a yoke of slavery. Galatians 5:1

We're called to be free. But how free?

In our culture, many believe freedom is the ability to do anything you want whenever you want. But when you live that way, you don't necessarily feel truly free. True freedom is in a life of faith in Christ.

Galatians 5:13 tells us to serve one another in love instead of indulging in flesh and selfish desires. Matthew 22 tells us to love the Lord our God with all hearts and love our neighbor as ourselves.

In these commands, it seems like we have a lot of freedom. The law of the Spirit is rooted in loving obedience to the God of grace. The law of Moses only signifies our guilt. The gospel of grace delivers us from slavery to the law and its condemnation. In Christ, we are free, and there is no condemnation (Rom. 8:1).

Freedom in Christ is not for us to see how much we can get away with. Instead, it's the freedom to bear the fruit of love for one another. However, actions and how we act out our faith is not a measure of our identity in Christ. Only the inward washing of the Spirit sets us free, and in that freedom we find our true identity.

It's a beautiful truth: Christ sets us free from sins. I know that freedom myself and have been transformed by the reality of this verse.

How have you been transformed by the gospel of grace?

Day 50 Linger

Day 51

Observe how Christ loved us. His love was not cautious but extravagant. He didn't love in order to get something from us but to give everything of himself to us. Love like that. Ephesians 5:2 (Msg)

Our God, Creator of the universe, has written an enormous and lovingly elaborate story of love, provision, and salvation for us, His people. He has a track record of faithfulness and mercy that reaches back far before us – and far beyond us. Sometimes we lose sight of how present God's love is for us daily. And how important it is that we receive it so that we can give it.

God spared nothing to show us how much He loves us. He sent his Son, Jesus. Our Savior never stopped loving. He never chose hatred or contempt, never shamed those that betrayed Him. When hard-pressed on every side, Jesus never resented the sacrifice He chose to make on our behalf. John 13:1 tells us that He loved to the end.

It's so easy to feel loved and to love when all seems right in our world. But what about those days when we feel unloved or rejected? I've lived a lot of life and have experienced the sting of both. When I began to realize the longsuffering and mercy of God and received His love in a pivotal season, my heart became whole, truly accepting how loved I am by Him.

God wants us to know every day, every moment who we are. When you open your heart, His love changes your mind. What if we began today embracing God's love for us – just as we are? When we do, we'll be able to show the world around us the purest love.

Jesus loved extravagantly. And He loves you, extravagantly. This love isn't elusive. It isn't pie-in-the-sky, out-of-reach, nor relegated to a few. It's real, and it's for you and me. Jesus raised the bar of love to extraordinary heights.

How can you raise the bar of love today in how you interact with others?

Day 51 Linger

Day 52

Don't fret or worry. Instead of worrying, pray. Let petitions and praises shape your worries into prayers, letting God know your concerns. Before you know it, a sense of God's wholeness, everything coming together for good, will come and settle you down. It's wonderful what happens when Christ displaces worry at the center of your life. Philippians 4:6-7 (Msg)

The primary battle we fight each day is the battle for our thoughts. As we begin a new day, will we allow our feelings to govern our minds and our environment? Or will we allow the truths of the Word of God to pierce through every lie of the enemy? Praying God's Word and praising in the middle of the unknown is a weapon to fight with, our shelter to run to, and the shield that guards our hearts – a powerful way to live. It turns anxiety into peace, brings chaos into order, and turns fear into faith.

We may be struggling and weary, not feeling like it. Recalling God's love and concern, and prayer and praise have the power to change our hearts and shift our circumstances.

Colossians 2:7 says, "Let your roots grow down into Him, and let your lives be built on Him. Then your faith will grow strong in the truth you were taught, and you will overflow with thankfulness."

The more our lives are rooted in Christ, the greater the life-giving strength we gain, and we become less consumed by circumstance. Gratitude is a powerful weapon that transforms our days and our future. It helps unlock what God has for us and helps us to think and live from Heaven's perspective.

Day 52 Linger

PRAISE AND RECALL

CONFESS

ASK

REST AND RECEIVE

Day 53

Let us hold fast the confession of our hope without wavering, for he who promised is faithful. And let us consider how to stir up one another to love and good works. Hebrews 10:23-24 (ESV)

How do you hold onto hope?

God's faithfulness isn't contingent upon our ability to always feel hopeful. I'm grateful for that because sometimes my hope is inconsistent. It can waver when I'm tired or weary.

Fortunately, Hebrews doesn't say we hold onto hope because we're good at it. It means we hold onto hope because Christ has been faithful. The blood of Jesus, His faithfulness – this is why we hold onto hope.

Whether or not you're in a season of joy or grief, full or empty, exciting or mundane – Christ's birth and life intersects your circumstances with steady, unwavering hope. The letter of Hebrews is written to Christians who were the subject of persecution. One of the primary purposes of the book is to encourage readers to persevere.

Because of God's love and presence, and because of Jesus, you can have freedom, boldness, and confidence.

It's easy to let delay diminish our faith. But, there is One who satisfies, and His hope lives within us. It's easy to set our hopes and dreams on things that don't ultimately fulfill our souls. God created you with a purpose and plan in mind that fulfills you like nothing, and no one can. If you're living in the 'not now' or 'not yet,' God knows exactly what's ahead for you, and He's making a way.

Day 53 Linger

PRAISE AND RECALL

CONFESS

ASK

REST AND RECEIVE

Day 54

But we do not belong to those who shrink back and are destroyed, but to those who have faith and are saved. Hebrews 10:39

Have you ever felt like you were wading in deep waters? Perhaps from something God called you to do or something pressing in your life, requiring you to trust God in a deeper level of surrender or trust. I have. Was it scary? Yes. Was God faithful? Yes.

I'm certain most everyone could answer yes to that question. Reflecting on overwhelming concerns in times past when I've had to persevere, I can see where God was building my character and faith. Where there was lack, He met with provision.

Don't be discouraged by what your eyes can't see yet. There is always hope, no matter what. What you see today isn't your entire story. There is so much more. Your obedience and prayers are sowing seed for your future. Don't stop. Don't give up. Keep pressing in.

Day 54 Linger

PRAISE AND RECALL

CONFESS

ASK

REST AND RECEIVE

Day 55

And the God of all grace, who called you to his eternal glory in Christ, after you have suffered a little while, will himself restore you and make you strong, firm, and steadfast. 1 Peter 5:10

It's true that in this world, we are going to suffer. Spiritual battles are going on that he wants us to remember. First, we have a very real enemy. And one of his most tactical moves is our tendency toward distraction. When facing pain and suffering often, we look for ways to make sense of it, ignore it, or numb it – anything but lean into it.

Are we surprised by suffering? The enemy would far rather us be surprised that we as Christians will go through suffering, especially if it causes us to doubt the goodness of God. Our pain and suffering are not an exception (1 Peter 4:12). And our struggles are not really with one another; they are with principalities that are against us and what God has for our lives (Ephesians 6:12).

Our enemy will use every arsenal to tear us away from the path God has called us on. He wants to keep us from becoming who God has created us to be – one who displays God's love and splendor to the world.

But here's the excellent news and the most important thing to remember: Jesus Christ defeated death and evil itself (John 16:33). We belong to an all-powerful God. In our suffering, He draws us closer, heals, and transforms despite it. Suffering is only temporary. Our salvation in Christ is secure, and God Himself will restore us and make us strong.

When the enemy tries to convince you that your story stops where your stress begins, when you feel like you'll never see the breakthrough, and when you feel too broken, know God is with you. He is for you. He can overcome every adversity. And He tenderly cares for you. Always.

Day 55 Linger

Praise and Recall

Confess

Ask

Rest and Receive

Day 56 Pause and Ponder

Day 57

The world and its desires pass away, but the man who does the will of God lives forever. 1 John 2:17

The comforts of this world are enticing. John is teaching us in 1 John that everything we take delight in this world will fade and is passing away. We shouldn't tie ourselves to it, or hold on too tight.

John isn't questioning the beauty of sunrise or sunset. He's not challenging the awe we feel when we gaze up at snow-topped mountains that appear as they're touching the sky. He's not questioning the glory of embracing a newborn baby. These things turn our affections toward God, our Creator. The world is made to be good, and God Himself called it very good indeed (Genesis 1:31).

Instead, he's speaking of things that pull our affections away from God; lust of the flesh, lust of the eyes, and pride.

We're all enticed, but we shouldn't tie ourselves to a ship that will ultimately sink. We have to make a choice. Our deepest affections should be reserved for God. We were created in love to love Him and others. His love is infinite and lasts forever, our hope and promises in Him are secure. He is our rock, treasure, and great reward.

Day 57 Linger

PRAISE AND RECALL

_____
_____
_____
_____
_____

CONFESS

_____
_____
_____
_____
_____

ASK

_____
_____
_____
_____
_____

REST AND RECEIVE

_____
_____
_____
_____

Day 58

This is how we know what love is: Jesus Christ laid down his life for us. And we ought to lay down our lives for our brothers. 1 John 3:16

John spent years learning and watching how Jesus loved people. He learned from the Master. In today's verse, we read his conclusion that we should love in action and truth. The love of Jesus is love in action. His active love wasn't limited to feeding the hungry, washing feet, going against cultural opinions to reach the outcasts, teaching the disciples how to fish. In love, He laid down His life for us. And in 1 John 3:16 He tells us that we should lay down our lives for one another.

Real love goes beyond our comfort, and often our willingness because it's hard. It can be really hard. It's sacrificial and can even be unpleasant. Jesus is the example of real love – He died for us.

When we're at our best, love can seem natural. But God calls us to love when no one is watching when it's the hardest. Loving God's way is selfless and sacrificial.

How can we follow the example of Jesus?

We love in His strength because "he remains in us." Our own strength will never be enough, but His call to love comes with a promise that He is with us to the end.

Day 58 Linger

PRAISE AND RECALL

CONFESS

ASK

REST AND RECEIVE

Day 59

This is how God showed his love among us: He sent his one and only Son into the world that we might live through him. 1 John 4:9

We have a deep longing for Jesus. Every human heart does. We have a space that only He can fill with His goodness, love, and peace. The One that came invites us to come - to Himself, to live life freely the way He intended. Jesus, the Son of God – the image of invisible God, breathed our air, felt our pain, knew our sorrows, died for our sins, and conquered death.

There are a million things that can capture our thoughts and daunt our to-do lists in daily living. How are you doing today? Are you hurried and distracted, or are you finding rhythms of grace and peace?

Encourage and permit yourself to scratch off things on your list this week that don't matter in the grand scheme.

Day 59 Linger

PRAISE AND RECALL

_____
_____
_____
_____
_____

CONFESS

_____
_____
_____
_____
_____

ASK

_____
_____
_____
_____
_____

REST AND RECEIVE

_____
_____
_____
_____

Day 60

And this is love: that we walk in obedience to his commands. As you have heard from the beginning, his command is that you walk in love. 2 John 6

The flurry of day to day life here on earth can cause us to forget what's real, true, and eternal. We get distracted and forget what's most important. There's a lot to be said in running the race before us with endurance toward Jesus. But here in this letter by John, he emphasizes the basics of following Christ – walking in truth and love.

The love of Jesus is like no other. You don't have to earn it. And there's nothing you can do to make Him stop loving you.

Love. We all want it, and we are commanded to give it and live it. To walk in love is to match our stride to the love of God, who sent Jesus to show us real love and to teach us how to love. True love always goes beyond receiving. It gives. It sacrifices. It unifies.

How can you sync your steps with His today and walk in more of His love?

Day 60 Linger

Praise and Recall

Confess

Ask

Rest and Receive

Part 3

A Full Life In The Emptiest Places: Presence In The Pause

Part 3 Introduction

I will always show you where to go. I'll give you a full life in the emptiest of places - firm muscles, strong bones. You'll be like a well-watered garden, a gurgling spring that never runs dry. You'll use the old rubble of past lives to build anew, rebuild the foundations from out of your past. Isaiah 58:11-12 (MSG)

There's not one of us that doesn't go through a season of empty – a wilderness season. It's in the wilderness that we are prepared for what's ahead. God isn't punishing you; He's preparing you.

When we go through a holding pattern, it doesn't mean that God is holding out on us. He's always at work preparing our hearts and our foundation to handle His purposes.

All of us have greatness for our lives. But it's the questions, barrenness, and difficulties that are our training ground for shoring up faith and confidence in God.

Even in the seasons you don't understand, they're all purposeful in His plan.

In nature, there is an emerging and blossoming that only happens when winter meets spring. There is a tension between the seen and the unseen. New growth and new life forms and pauses patiently below the surface until the atmosphere above ground can sustain it and cause it to flourish.

The desire to flourish is deep within every living thing and every created being. When we study nature, we see that most of what coaxes life from seed to bloom to flourishing is nourishment. Being wholly surrounded by soil and saturated with water, the germination process yields new life breaking through the ground at its appointed time.

Day 61

"Let us break their chains and throw off their shackles", they say. The One enthroned in heaven laughs; the Lord scoffs at them. Psalm 2:3-4

This Psalm describes the coming of Christ to establish His eternal reign. Recent and current world events highlight more than ever how much we are not in control and how much we need to have confidence in God. Crises help us discover what we believe and where we have questions about our faith.

I've learned firsthand that crises don't relegate the goodness of God; they are an opportunity to discover His goodness. Today's struggles disappointments and difficulties don't tell our whole story. There is always a bigger picture.

There's no better place to learn the vocabulary of prayer than in the book of Psalm. God's people have used psalms as a guide for worship and prayer since before the time of Christ. They help us find words to express ourselves to God in every circumstance.

Everyone serves somebody and something. Too often, people think they will be free if they can get away from God. The truth is, only surrender brings true freedom. Only God can set us free.

Verse 4 tells us that the One enthroned in Heaven laughs. Here God isn't laughing at the nations, but at their confused thoughts about power. He knows their limited strength, and He knows His power.

Continue reading Psalm 2 on your own, and you see that in obedience, there would be a blessing. We can live in a realm of peace and hope because God is faithful and gives us strength. One day at a time. To the very end.

Day 61 Linger

PRAISE AND RECALL

CONFESS

ASK

REST AND RECEIVE

Day 62

In peace I will lie down and sleep, for you alone, Lord, make me dwell in safety. Psalm 4:8

We long for a life filled with peace and purpose, and there are seasons when we have to wait for God's plan to unfold. We wait, watch, and hope. We want to believe Him. Hope can fade in the waiting or in stacking disappointments. The unseen can make us weary and cause us to shrink back.

Shrinking back isn't what God intended for our lives. While there is breath in your lungs, there is hope – the promise of a new day.

Are you waiting for something?

Perhaps a relationship to be restored, financial breakthrough, a job situation to shift, a child to be conceived. Whatever your specific situation is today, know that God can be trusted to provide for your needs and will help you walk in His plan for your life. Trusting in His faithfulness day by day increases our ability to persevere and live in peace.

God invites us into the unseen for intimacy with Him. It's in this place where hope grows, which produces faith and belief. It's one of God's foundational promises for us. The unseen isn't intended to make us fear. It's an opportunity for us to know and trust God's heart more.

Lamentations 3:22-24 tells us the Lord's compassions never fail and are new every morning. Is there an area you need to receive His peace and rest today?

Day 62 Linger

Praise and Recall

Confess

Ask

Rest and Receive

Day 63 Pause and Ponder

Day 64

Give ear to my words, O Lord, consider my sighing. Listen to my cry for help, my King and my God, for to you I pray. In the morning, O Lord you hear my voice; in the morning I lay my requests before you and wait in expectation. Psalm 5:1-3

I don't know for sure what enemy lies David was asking God to defend against in Psalm 5. David had a few enemies along the way that were out to destroy him. But he had discovered friendship and a strong relationship with God, and he knew God would protect him. His relationship with God was one of confidence and expectation because he knew Him intimately. He found the secret of a close relationship was in talking to Him, praying to Him earnestly.

If your eyes are open, if your heart is beating, you know that life can bring heartache. Relationships can become broken. Injustice happens. At some point, something and someone will come against you. But here is the beautiful thing about our God: He hears every single prayer. He is the One we can turn to in every situation, and He is the One that can do something about it.

> Confidence in God and expectation is the heart of David's prayer.

I can imagine David waking, sighing under the weight of a burden. But he rises and goes straight to God with his troubles. Have you ever started a day feeling weighed down? I have. I love how God gives us the psalms to help us have language and an example of how to bring it all to Him. Every situation. Every range of emotion.

Like David, you can safely and securely lay every burden down before the Lord today and expect His goodness.

Day 64 Linger

PRAISE AND RECALL

_____
_____
_____
_____
_____

CONFESS

_____
_____
_____
_____
_____

ASK

_____
_____
_____
_____
_____

REST AND RECEIVE

_____
_____
_____
_____

Day 65

In the Lord I take refuge, How then can you say to me: 'Flee like a bird to your mountain. For look, the wicked bend their bows; they set their arrows against the strings to shoot from the shadows at the upright in heart. When the foundations are being destroyed, what can the righteous do?' The Lord is in His holy temple; the Lord is on His heavenly throne. He observes the sons of me; His eyes examine them. Psalm 11:1-4

David had to flee for safety several times in his life. Being God's anointed king didn't make him immune to injustice and pursuit of his enemies. In Psalm 11, we see that David was in a crisis. He seems to be speaking to those who are advising him to run from his enemies.

Here we see that David's faith contrasted dramatically with the fear of the advisers who were telling him to flee. The size of the enemy and the problem was their focus. In verse 4, we see that David's focus on the strength and power of his God.

Verse 3 refers to foundations being destroyed. Here the word foundation means social order. Social order was being shaken, and David was advised to run away and hide in the mountains. If David were to leave, it would have been safer for him, but the social order would have collapsed. Instead of running, David took a stand and stayed put, honored God, and did what was best for the people amid distress and danger. He knew God was greater than anything his enemies could bring against him.

> Faith in God helps us resist fear and keeps us from losing hope.

If we only look at what is going on around us, life can feel out of control, and fear can set in. But we have to remember we have never been in control in the first place. The foundations of the world begin and end with God. He has a plan. He is still governing. And He is still ruling.

Any turn of events does not diminish God's power. Nothing is outside of His reach. Even in the most challenging times in your life, you can experience the intimate presence of God. These moments we're living in can be used for our good by God and are an opportunity to grow in an even greater understanding of God's love, strength, and peace.

Day 65 Linger

PRAISE AND RECALL

CONFESS

ASK

REST AND RECEIVE

Day 66

The LORD looks down from heaven on all mankind to see if there are any who understand, any who seek God. Psalm 14:2

Giving someone the keys to something you value greatly is a great act of trust and kindness. Keys usually represent access. To be given the 'keys of the kingdom' means to be given access to God. Through His death and resurrection, Jesus gave us access. He made a way in the greatest display of love and mercy; on the cross.

The message of Psalm 14 is nearly identical to Psalm 53. Psalm 14 is practical; Psalm 53 is prophetic. Psalm 14 deals with the past, Psalm 53, with the future.

Everyone faces challenges in their lives. But the good news is, God not only looks for those who seek Him, but also leans in close and is our strength when we do. He provides a safe place no matter what we face. The kingdom of God goes beyond just what He does in our lives. It's also about what He does through us for His glory and the benefit of others. It involves seeking God and seeking justice for the poor. Psalm 14 ends on this note.

God has always and still does look for those who seek Him. Because of Jesus, we have the privilege of prayer and seeking God. He can be sought and found when we seek Him wholeheartedly. And in Him, we find strength. wisdom, peace, rest, and life.

Day 66 Linger

PRAISE AND RECALL

_____
_____
_____
_____
_____

CONFESS

_____
_____
_____
_____
_____

ASK

_____
_____
_____
_____
_____

REST AND RECEIVE

_____
_____
_____
_____

Day 67

In you our ancestors put their trust; they trusted and you delivered them. Psalm 22:4

David is writing out of a wounded heart of rejection in this Psalm. Yet, he believed that God would lead him out of despair. It's a prayer that carries us from great suffering to great joy.

Rejection stings. We've all faced it at some point. But one of the many beautiful things about knowing God is that God's love, concern, and plans for us aren't limited by or to what we experience in our life on earth. It reaches back to when He first created us and reaches into eternity.

In this Psalm, David once again poured out his honest questions and his anguish to God. One of the first things that stand out to me in the book of Psalm is how, when inviting God into the honest questions, doubts, and fears, there is a shift in the soul of the writers. It's just as relevant today as it was when these psalms were written. Too often, we keep the hard stuff bottled up. It's dangerous to do that because it opens the door for sin and defeat, depression, and bitterness to take root.

There was a time when my life became turbulent beyond what I had known - deaths, loss, friendship betrayals. What I didn't know firsthand then was that God could handle my deep despair, my disappointment. I felt hopeless and didn't know how pivotal and powerful it can be to cry out to God amid anguish. It wouldn't have immediately changed my circumstances, but it sure would have changed my heart and perspective. Bitterness took root as I suppressed and just tried to cope. It got the best of me for a season. I gave up. And then, one day, God met me powerfully and pivotally through Psalm 22.

God's deliverance, when I was at my lowest, changed everything.

Because of this, I can tell you with full confidence; there is no despair, disappointment, hurt, sin, or loss that He can't help you overcome. Next time you feel a sting of rejection or hurt, keep in mind the hope and victory that God has already promised you.

Day 67 Linger

Praise and Recall

_____
_____
_____
_____
_____

Confess

_____
_____
_____
_____
_____

Ask

_____
_____
_____
_____
_____

Rest and Receive

_____
_____
_____
_____

Day 68

Test me, Lord, and try me, examine my heart and my mind. Psalm 26:2

We note in Psalm 26 David declaring his loyalty to God and that despite the danger he was facing, he remained confident that God would help him securely stand in an even place.

David wrote this psalm in a time of trouble, like much of what He wrote. It opens in verse 1, with his request for God to vindicate him, presumably from his enemies. The invitation itself implies that David wasn't able to defend himself or that he chose not to; confident that God would answer his prayer. Despite his present difficulty, he had the confidence to say, "I shall not slip".

In verse 2, David invites the Lord to examine him. He was confident enough in his demonstrated life of faith that he asked God to consider his heart. David had learned through his failures and troubles of God's mercy, His lovingkindness. He had learned that God can always be trusted.

In this passage, the request to be examined refers to the inward working – the mind and the heart. David knew the importance of both a pure inner life and right actions and deeds. Inviting God into the deepest part of our inward hearts and minds is an excellent path to freedom and victory.

He also knew the value of sustained examination and meditation upon the lovingkindness of God.

Reflecting on the goodness, mercy, kind love of God helps us see Him and His goodness in our lives, which also helps increase our faith and ability to trust Him in any situation and season. When we let God examine us, it makes room to shift our perspectives to His ways and thoughts. It's not to control us. It's about options - freedom. Culture says surrender means defeat and weakness. But in God's economy, submission is where true liberty begins.

It's a beautiful exchange: Replacing chaos with His order and replacing fear with faith. Replacing worry with worship.

Having a right walk with God meant more to David than just avoiding evil. He had a pure, simple, yet deep love for God and His presence and was able to declare the victory before he experienced it!

This psalm ends repeating David's resolve of trust in God. Despite the dangers around him in verse 12, he declares, "My feet stand on level ground; in the great assembly, I will praise the Lord."

God's lovingkindness is sure, faithful, and goes into the smallest of your details. Dwelling on it is a great place to start each day.

Amid adversity, is the time to be awake for what the Lord is doing. The rough ground is a picture of life's trials. We are not immune to them, but they never need to shake us - because our God is unshakeable.

Day 68 Linger

PRAISE AND RECALL

_____
_____
_____
_____
_____

CONFESS

_____
_____
_____
_____
_____

ASK

_____
_____
_____
_____
_____

REST AND RECEIVE

_____
_____
_____
_____

Day 69

I remain confident of this: I will see the goodness of the Lord in the land of the living. Psalm 27:13

Waiting for God, for answers to prayers, isn't easy. But God and His timing are worth waiting for. Have you ever had to wait? I have. We all have. Think back to when you had to wait on God for something; a deep-felt prayer need, healing, next steps. The list could go on. After a season of waiting, what did you discover about God and His timing? One thing I have learned is that His delay does not always mean denial.

> Sometimes we wait because God is preparing us for His answers. Sometimes we have to wait because He's preparing others for His answers to our prayers. In the waiting is where we get to discover more about God and his heart for us and our loved ones.

Lamentations 3:24-26 calls us to hope in and wait for the Lord because often God will use our season of waiting to refresh, renew, and teach us.

David had such confidence in and desire for God and His Presence. David was a skilled warrior, but he learned to look to the Lord for his strength while waiting on God to deliver and rescue him.

We can find it easy to trust in our skills, wisdom, experience, friends, and resources. It's easy to slip into that mindset when things are rolling along, but nothing can sustain us like the strength of the Lord. David knew a greater strength than his own, and his confidence in God was battle-tested. He knew something of what the Apostle Paul would write many years later in Ephesians 6:10, "Be strong in the Lord and in the power of His might."

God reveals His richness to the seeking heart, the waiting heart. David's seeking after God and his knowledge of the Lord lead him to this triumphant declaration. The idea behind waiting on the Lord isn't a passive sitting around. God gives us strength as we seek Him and rely on Him, instead of relying on our own strength.

Day 69 Linger

Praise and Recall

_____
_____
_____
_____
_____

Confess

_____
_____
_____
_____
_____

Ask

_____
_____
_____
_____
_____

Rest and Receive

_____
_____
_____
_____

Day 70 Pause and Ponder

Day 71

Then I acknowledged my sin to you and did not cover up my iniquity. I said, "I will confess my transgressions to the Lord." And you forgave the guilt of my sin. Psalm 32:5

Do you ever find it hard to forgive? It could be others or even yourself. In today's passage, we see the very high cost and massive blessing of God's forgiveness. When you have experienced God's forgiveness you, it becomes easier to forgive others and yourself.

God has made total forgiveness available to you and me through Jesus. In Psalm 32, we see a huge difference that God's forgiveness makes. In verses 3 and 4, David describes the spiritual agony of not being forgiven. After he sinned, David says 'I kept silent.' That's when the trouble began. Observe in this Psalm what happens. He writes my bones wasted away—guilt ravages a person physically. David describes anguish in his soul that doesn't stop. He felt a distance between himself and God. Guilt skews our perception of who God is and His readiness to forgive us.

In this Psalm, David describes how to deal with guilt and seek forgiveness from God. When we acknowledge and confess our sins, it strips away pride and wrong attitudes, trying to 'dress up' what we've done. The Lord wants us to come as we are, no mask or pretense. When we take responsibility for what we've done and confess and cast it to God, He forgives.

At the end of Psalm 32, David can't help but shout for joy. He received forgiveness and a fresh start. Through the cross, God restores us to a right relationship with Him. He wants us to walk in His ways and trust in His love. Have you experienced God's forgiveness? Is there someone you need to forgive today? It could even be the need to forgive yourself.

Day 71 Linger

PRAISE AND RECALL

CONFESS

ASK

REST AND RECEIVE

Day 72

Blessed are those whose strength is in you, who have set their hearts on pilgrimage. As they pass through the Valley of Baca, they make it a place of springs; the autumn rains also cover it with pools. They go from strength to strength, till each appears before God in Zion. Psalm 84:5-7

Baca means mourning or weeping. Notice the phrase in today's verse, 'as they pass through' in verse 6. They had to pass through a barren place on their pilgrimage to the temple. God doesn't waste any part of our journey, no matter what barrenness we must go through.

The enemy's whispers and lies can cause us to question God. But you have the choice to choose and act on what you believe.

> Discovering more profound things of God requires deeper faith, deeper valleys, deeper resolve. Without delays, we wouldn't know how to hope for the unseen, and we would never experience the faithfulness of God in the waiting. Your revelation of God forms the basis of expectation, which leads to realization. You live your life based on your revelation of God.

Be encouraged today, if you set your heart on the Lord, you will receive strength upon strength in every adversity; and as you pass through, barren places will become well-watered and used for your good.

Day 72 Linger

PRAISE AND RECALL

CONFESS

ASK

REST AND RECEIVE

Day 73

Do you not know? Have you not heard? The Lord is the everlasting God, the Creator of the ends of the earth. He will not grow tired or weary, and his understanding no one can fathom. Isaiah 40:28

Has God call ever called you to do something and you didn't understand what it meant, why, or the timing? If so, you're in good company. Many in the Bible experienced that kind of call or instruction from the Lord. Moses, Noah, Mary, for starters.

Sometimes following God is risky. Not because He's not faithful. But because it costs us something.

I recall God calling us back to Austin, Texas. It felt risky. Our business and friendships were stable and established. We were comfortable. But we knew without a doubt, God spoke with vision and clarity. And we had learned that following His isn't about our comfort. Some days were exhausting in the natural but our souls were at rest because we had experienced the faithfulness of God.

To step into a place of trust, first, we have to learn to be quiet, be still and willing to let go. We can't afford to have a thought about our lives that God does not. Faith is looking past the landscape of your circumstances to the restoration God has promised on the horizon.

> Seasons shift, but it may take a minute for the external to catch up with the internal.

God is never out of time. For all the things you think should have happened by now – there's still time. He is not limited by our clock. God is not limited to age or cultural definitions and expectations.

When God created you, He made you for purpose and impact. Take time today to reflect on your dreams and hopes. Have you made them about you? Or are you fully submitted to how and when God unfolds them?

When your dreams or hopes make you anxious, they disrupt the Lordship of Jesus in your life. He tells us, Be anxious for nothing. But in everything in prayer and supplication, make your request known (Philippians 4:6).

Day 73 Linger

PRAISE AND RECALL
_____
_____
_____
_____
_____

CONFESS
_____
_____
_____
_____
_____

ASK
_____
_____
_____
_____
_____

REST AND RECEIVE
_____
_____
_____

Day 74

But, this is what the Lords says - He who created you, Jacob, He who formed you, Israel: Do not fear, for I have redeemed you; I have summoned you by name; you are mine. Isaiah 43:1

When the enemy tries to convince you that your story stops here.
This is what the Lord says.
When you feel like you'll never see the breakthrough.
This is what the Lord says.
When you feel too broken.
This is what the Lord says.

Do not fear.

God's goodness toward you is unceasing. I love how this verse starts with, "But this is what the Lord says."

God redeemed Israel and summoned them by name to be those who belong to Him. God protected Israel in times of trouble. He still protects today and summons those that belong to Him by name.

God's love is greater and higher than any opposition you will ever face.

He gives strength for victory. Your God is faithful. Let the weight of His promises sink in today. Watch for the miracles. Look and be ready for them. Take the risk to trust God.

Day 74 Linger

PRAISE AND RECALL

CONFESS

ASK

REST AND RECEIVE

Day 75

Shout for joy, you heavens; rejoice, you earth; burst into song, you mountains! For the Lord comforts his people and will have compassion on his afflicted ones. Isaiah 49:13

We live in a generation where our lives have become so instantaneous that anything that requires perseverance and patience can appear unattractive. We expect instant returns and instant results. But sometimes the most significant pay-offs and breakthroughs take a long time.

In Romans 12:11, Paul admonishes us to keep our spiritual fervor, to be as enthusiastic as the day we first encountered Jesus. Do you recall that day?

In Galatians 6:9, scripture encourages us not to become weary in doing good because, at the proper time, we'll reap a harvest. There are many reasons we can feel like giving up. When we don't see results immediately or after a long season of sowing, it's easy to become discouraged. Sometimes it's when you look back years later that you can see the seed sown has become a harvest. Keeping an eternal perspective helps us to stay positive. Some seeds we sow, we'll never know anything about until we reach heaven.

In Isaiah, we read that Isaiah waited on God to speak to him so that he would know the right words to encourage the weary – those who were tempted to give up (Isaiah 50:4).

No matter how long it takes to see results you are praying and hoping for, if you abide and hope in the Lord scripture assures us we won't be disappointed. We are walking testaments of God's grace and mercy in a dying world.

> When we follow Jesus, the way we love and live stands out in a fallen world.

Day 75 Linger

PRAISE AND RECALL

_____
_____
_____
_____
_____
_____

CONFESS

_____
_____
_____
_____
_____
_____

ASK

_____
_____
_____
_____
_____
_____

REST AND RECEIVE

_____
_____
_____
_____

Day 76

But blessed is the man who trusts in the Lord, whose confidence is in him. He will be like a tree planted by the water that sends out its roots by the stream. It does not fear when heat comes; its leaves are always green. It has no worries in a year of drought and never fails to bear fruit. Jeremiah 17:8

There is an emerging and blossoming that only happens when winter meets spring. There is a tension between the seen and the unseen. New growth and new life forms and pauses patiently below the surface until the atmosphere above ground can sustain it and cause it to flourish. New life remains unseen until its season arrives. That doesn't mean it was any less alive.

The desire to flourish is deep within every living thing and every created being. When we study nature, we see that most of what coaxes life from a seed to bloom to flourishing is nourishment. Being wholly surrounded by soil and saturated with water, the germination process yields new life breaking through the ground at its appointed time.

> Delays in life are inevitable and sometimes intentional by
> God in order to make room for and prepare us for His plans.

Have you ever been in the middle of a great big causing you to make a choice to keep trusting God? I have been in circumstance that caused me to question His quality as Father and anxiety became the natural temptation. But I have learned when I make the choice to believe truths about His love for me, what's spoken over my life and His ability to accomplish it, I find peace in the pauses of life.

Day 76 Linger

PRAISE AND RECALL

_____
_____
_____
_____
_____

CONFESS

_____
_____
_____
_____
_____

ASK

_____
_____
_____
_____
_____

REST AND RECEIVE

_____
_____
_____
_____

Day 77 Pause and Ponder

Day 78

For the revelation awaits an appointed time; it speaks of the end and will not prove false. Though it linger, wait for it; it will certainly come and will not delay. Habakkuk 2:3

Have you ever been through a season that felt like answers would never come? Or have you felt like you were far off from all that God had promised? I know I have. Through this time, God was teaching me to recall His promises, to believe, and to live with an attitude of expectation.

Habakkuk, a prophet, was a man who sought answers. Troubled by what he observed, he asked difficult questions because what he saw in a dying world broke his heart. He boldly took his complaints and questions directly to God.

Are you feeling stuck? Habakkuk sure did. And so have I.

God wants us to come to Him with our struggles and doubts. When we choose to trust God for His timing, He gives sustains us and gives us strength. God is for you. Trusting Him leads to peace and quiet hope.

Day 78 Linger

PRAISE AND RECALL

CONFESS

ASK

REST AND RECEIVE

Day 79

He got up, rebuked the wind and said to the waves, "Quiet! Be still!"
Then the wind died down and it was completely calm. Mark 4:39

In Mark 4, we read where Jesus invited the disciples to get in a boat with Him to go to the other side of the lake so they could rest. While they were crossing the lake, Jesus was sleeping, and a violent, unexpected storm came up and broke over the boat. The disciples were terrified and panicked. Waking Jesus up, they questioned His care for them. Jesus responded to their cries and immediately rebuked the winds.

One of the interesting things about this story that's not talked about much is that when Jesus invited the disciples into the boat, He knew there would be a storm. Have you ever stopped to think about that? Jesus invited the disciples into the boat to go across the lake to rest, knowing there would be a storm ahead. But He knew His authority over that storm and was actually sleeping in the bottom of the boat when it squalled.

The disciples lived with Jesus, yet they underestimated Him. They had seen what He could do, and they still panicked in a crisis. Can you relate to how they reacted? I think most of us can. How often do we face adversity and surrender to stress, forgetting what we've seen God do or know that He can do?

The same power of Jesus that calmed that storm still applies to the winds of our lives, and He wants to use it to calm you in your very own situation.

Spend some time today remembering and rehearsing what you want to recall about God, His promises, power, and authority in your life when turbulent times come.

Day 79 Linger

PRAISE AND RECALL

CONFESS

ASK

REST AND RECEIVE

Day 80

The angel went to her and said, "Greetings, you who are highly favored! The Lord is with you. Luke 1:28

Some two thousand years ago, the Israelites had been waiting centuries for the coming of the Savior – God's son, Jesus Christ. And, He was birthed through Mary - young, poor, female - all characteristics that, to the people of her day, would make her seem unusable by God for any significant task. But God chose Mary for one of the most important acts of obedience he has ever demanded of anyone.

In Luke 1, the angel, Gabriel, made two appearances and made two announcements. One appearance was to Zechariah, and one was to Mary. He appeared to Zechariah to bring news that his wife Elizabeth would bear a son, John. He appeared to Mary to deliver news that she would birth a son, Jesus.

Both were announcements and promises spoken into unlikely and impossible situations. The first words Gabriel spoke to both Zechariah and Mary was 'Do not be afraid'.

Same invitation. Yet, we read about two different responses.

Zechariah replied, 'How can I be sure of this?' in verse 18.

Mary replied with 'How will this be?' in verse 34.

Zechariah doubted. Mary was expectant. She didn't have all of the answers. But she said yes. She risked not being believed by her fiancé Joseph and misunderstood and even ridiculed by all who knew her. Even though Mary and Zechariah had two different responses, they were both on a journey to know and experience the heart of God and His promises unfolding.

God is a God of order and process, and He loves us so much that He is willing to invite us into a journey with Him to know Him deeper - every day, every season.

He is the only way and real strength to say 'yes' even when we don't understand. Yes, because he is God, and He is good. He is faithful to keep his promises.

Is there an area you need to release to Him today in a process? Is there a question or a calling where you need to say, 'Yes, God, I trust you.'

Day 80 Linger

Praise and Recall

_____
_____
_____
_____
_____

Confess

_____
_____
_____
_____
_____

Ask

_____
_____
_____
_____
_____

Rest and Receive

_____
_____
_____

Day 81

The Lord is with you.' Mary was greatly troubled at his words and wondered what kind of greeting this might be. But the angel said to her, 'Do not be afraid, Mary; you have found favor with God. You will conceive and give birth to a son, and you are to call him Jesus.' Luke 1:29-30

Mary was chosen - highly favored because she believed. And through her, the Son of God would come - the world's only Hope. Yet she must have had days of being misunderstood, ridicule, doubt, fear, pain.

Her submission was part of God's plan to bring about our salvation. It's mind-blowing to me how the Savior invites us to be a part of the greater story. In comparison, our callings will never be as high as Mary's was; to birth, the Savior of the world. But we will all face challenges of moments between a promise and a promise fulfilled.

Have you ever experienced days asking God 'is this you or is it me?'. Did I hear from you?

When you doubt something God has spoken, stay close to Him. Ask Him. He speaks and confirms through His word, prayer, and others. God never intended those who walk with Him to feel comfortable and equipped. He only promised to be with us.

From the promise to the stable, what do you think life was like for Mary? How can you learn from her faith and act of obedience?

Day 81 Linger

PRAISE AND RECALL

_____
_____
_____
_____
_____

CONFESS

_____
_____
_____
_____
_____

ASK

_____
_____
_____
_____
_____

REST AND RECEIVE

_____
_____
_____
_____

Day 82

The Word became flesh and made his dwelling among us. We have seen his glory, the glory of the one and only Son, who came from the Father, full of grace and truth. John 1:14

We all long for home. By definition, home is the place where one lives permanently. John 1:1 tells us Jesus was fully human and fully God. We are create to be at home with Him eternally.

The Apostle John's words were written to prove conclusively that Jesus is the Son of God. He made the way for eternal life. They're not only words to open a new book in the Bible; they are the beginning of understanding who Jesus is. He is our promised Savior, the one who was with God from the start.

Jesus showed us how to live, a model of what we are to become. His life modeled grace and truth. Just as His Father gives us unmerited favor and unwavering.

Since the fall of man, every soul has longed for reconciliation with our Creator. The Son of God, Jesus, has always been the long-awaited Savior to redeem us.

You are a friend of Jesus. If you are a Believer, you are saved through His finished work on the cross. But who is Jesus to you? Take time to read through John 1 and let the truths of who He is sink into your soul.

Day 82 Linger

PRAISE AND RECALL

CONFESS

ASK

REST AND RECEIVE

Day 83

Therefore, since we have been justified through faith, we have peace with God through our Lord Jesus Christ, through whom we have gained access by faith into this grace in which we now stand.
Romans 5:1-2

There's no barrier between you and God. He broke down all obstacles through Jesus.

The essence of love is giving. The more a gift costs and the less the recipient deserves it, the greater is the love that gives. This is what God's love is for you.

Being able to stand in grace means we are friends of God, not enemies. Faith, hope, and love are at the heart of Christian life. Our relationship with God begins with faith. Hope grows as our faith increases and we learn all that God has in mind for us, giving us promise for our future. And God's love fills our lives overflowing to the world around us.

This is the gospel. It's what we live for. We can cling to and live by the love of the One who created us, saved us, and calls us His own.

Day 83 Linger

PRAISE AND RECALL

CONFESS

ASK

REST AND RECEIVE

Day 84 Pause and Ponder

Day 85

And we know that in all things God works for the good of those who love him, who have been called according to his purpose. Romans 8:28

Have you ever felt overwhelmed, overtired, or just over it?

In Romans 8, Paul shoots up a flare of truth for the Believer when feeling anxious, overwhelmed, or disoriented. If God can work all things for our good and His glory, then He can help us stand steady. God's promise in Romans 8:28 means He's already at work, reshaping every situation for our good. God can redeem every trial, every hardship in our lives. There's nothing beyond His reach now or in all of your tomorrows. Nothing can stop Him from working good in your life- not even you.

Life is big, and a lot happens across our years, but God's truth anchors us.

Nothing can stop the constant presence of God in our lives.

No illness or trial can keep us from our real source of life and strength in Him. God's purposes are always being worked out. Your season has not caught Him by surprise. In the waiting know He's not forgotten you. Praise in the pause, in the quiet, in the middle. It makes all the difference.

Day 85 Linger

PRAISE AND RECALL

CONFESS

ASK

REST AND RECEIVE

Day 86

May the God of hope fill you with all joy and peace as you trust in him, so that you may overflow with hope by the power of the Holy Spirit. Romans 15:13

God's peace is both a prayer and a promise. The more we know about what God has done in the past, the greater the confidence we have about what He will do in the future. Faith releases hope, joy, and peace in our lives. Doubt steals our joy and peace.

The reason for our hope is Jesus. The source of our hope comes from the Holy Spirit. The hope we have isn't wishful thinking. It comes from what God has done for us and is doing in us. Our ability to endure, persevere, and overcome is fueled by hope.

In God's peace, our souls are set free.

Free from perfection.

Free from needing approval from others.

Free from fear.

When we are full of His hope and peace, we become free from everything that would try to disrupt our confidence in God and what He's working out in our lives.

The hope for you, me, and the whole world is in Jesus. It's through scriptures we know about Jesus and the hope that is in Him. Studying scriptures regularly keeps us anchored. Take some time in the Linger section today and write out a scripture that helps strengthen your peace.

Day 86 Linger

PRAISE AND RECALL

_____
_____
_____
_____
_____

CONFESS

_____
_____
_____
_____
_____

ASK

_____
_____
_____
_____
_____

REST AND RECEIVE

_____
_____
_____
_____

Day 87

In all my prayers for all of you, I always pray with joy because of your partnership in the gospel from the first day until now, being confident of this, that he who began a good work in you will carry it on to completion until the day of Christ Jesus. Philippians 1:4-6

Don't let what you don't see yet diminish your vision and faith for what God has for your life. Most of the work God does is in the unseen, the quiet, and still seasons. It's in these moments we get to choose to let what we do know; His Word, Promises, what He has already spoken remind us that He sees the end from the beginning.

God can work through you in unexpected ways. We live in an age of unparalleled opportunities and mobility. Yet so many are unduly anxious about missing their destiny or taking a wrong step. But as a Believer, you can have confidence that because God began the good work in, you will be faithful to complete it. We are all works in progress.

When I'm discouraged by what I don't see yet, I remember that obedience is my part, and the results are in God's hands. The final responsibility is all God's. I love that.

Is there any area you need to replace confidence in yourself and what you can do with faith in Christ and what He will do?

Day 87 Linger

PRAISE AND RECALL

_____
_____
_____
_____
_____

CONFESS

_____
_____
_____
_____
_____

ASK

_____
_____
_____
_____
_____

REST AND RECEIVE

_____
_____
_____
_____

Day 88

For you died, and your life is now hidden with Christ in God. When Christ, who is your life appears, then you also will appear with him in glory. Colossians 3:3-4

How can we be encouraged to hold onto the promises and plans of God when we don't see Him working?

Sometimes we wait for an answer to a need. Sometimes we wait for an answer to a dream. These are two different types of delay, but how we view and trust God in the way we wait in each one makes all the difference in our peace, perspective, and expectancy.

To be hidden means concealed and safe. We are hidden in Christ, which means we are safe in Him. We're sons and daughters born with a God-given purpose, and we have a mission in this world. Don't let what you can't see diminish your vision and faith for what God has for your life. Delay does not decrease your purpose. Most of the work God does is in the unseen. It's in these moments we get to choose to let what we do know - His Word, His Promises, what He has already spoken - remind us that God sees the end from the beginning.

1 Corinthians 1:8-9 says, "He will also keep you firm to the end so that you will be blameless on the day of our Lord Jesus Christ. God is faithful, who has called you into fellowship with his Son, Jesus Christ, our Lord."

Today's struggles, disappointments, and difficulties don't tell the whole story. Keep in mind there is a bigger picture. We can live in a realm of peace and hope because God is faithful and gives us strength. One day at a time. To the very end.

Day 88 Linger

PRAISE AND RECALL

CONFESS

ASK

REST AND RECEIVE

Day 89

But you are a chosen people, a royal priesthood, a holy nation, God's special possession, that you may declare the praises of him who called you out of darkness into his wonderful light. 1 Peter 2:9

There is something else we all desperately need that can only be found in Christ. The birth of Jesus proclaims a message of salvation and hope, assuring us that God always fulfills His promises and that He uses ordinary people who love Him to do extraordinary things.

God created you for something significant. If your world sounds noisy today, take some time to be still. Remind yourself of who you are. Replace any lies you might be believing with truths from God's word. The only way to know what God is wanting to do or is doing in your life is to lean into His word presence. Ask what He is speaking over you.

We need life and hope, joy and peace, food and drink, satisfaction and salvation. He knows our needs better than we do, and He is willing to satisfy. He is able to satisfy. He loves us and gives us Himself, filling us up out of abundance and meeting our every need.

I pray the truths of God to come alive in you as you near the end of this ninety-day devotional - to heal the past, bind up wounds, and renew faith. Jesus is Emmanuel - God with us, and we are all part of His extraordinary story.

Day 89 Linger

PRAISE AND RECALL
_____
_____
_____
_____
_____

CONFESS
_____
_____
_____
_____
_____

ASK
_____
_____
_____
_____
_____

REST AND RECEIVE
_____
_____
_____
_____

Day 90

This is how God showed his love among us: He sent his one and only Son into the world that we might live through him. 1 John 4:9

Jesus' birth was only the first step in God's plan of salvation. God was preparing a way to redeem the human race. Since the fall of mankind He had already been preparing the way — but now He was taking on human flesh and becoming a man so that we could be saved. In time, that process would be completed through Jesus' death and resurrection — but at first, His plan was almost invisible.

Jesus came in a way unexpected: born of a virgin in a stable. His birth was announced first to the least likely; humble shepherds who were looked down upon by many.

Jesus Christ came for all people – rich and poor, male and female, uneducated, and educated. God demonstrated His great love for every one of us.

I want to live postured to hear and respond like Mary and the shepherds did - willing to respond to the Father's heart to do what's next—fully surrendered. Man, by nature, tends to choose the path of what seems rational - but God chooses the path of least likelihood.

Sometimes we feel like the Lord's plan is invisible. How can you learn from Mary's and the shepherds' response to the Lord?

Lord, help us to abide in your presence today. Please help us to trust in you in the unexpected and unexplainable.

Day 90 Linger

PRAISE AND RECALL

_____
_____
_____
_____
_____

CONFESS

_____
_____
_____
_____
_____

ASK

_____
_____
_____
_____
_____

REST AND RECEIVE

_____
_____
_____

exhale

About the Author

Holly Newton is passionate about inspiring women to freely live in their full purpose through encountering God's presence and the power of the Holy Spirit. A Bible teacher and mentor marked by authenticity and vulnerability, she encourages women to study Scripture, ask the hard questions, and get to know God's voice to more fully live out their purpose.

Holly studied at Baylor University and married her high school sweetheart Mark. Texas is home though they enjoyed five years living in Nashville, Tennessee.

Holly is Founder and Visionary of Exhale Women, which was birthed in Nashville. Exhale Women exists to encourage and equip the everyday woman to find and live out her purpose through knowing God – discovering her true identity. The inaugural Exhale Weekend struck a deep need in the hearts of women to rest, receive, and connect. It has doubled and tripled every year, and the ministry of Exhale Women expects a record-breaking number for the gathering in November 2020.

Holly and Mark have three young adult children – all married, and seven grandchildren – six on earth and one with Jesus.

Hi Friend,

Like you, I need community. It doesn't just happen. We have to make intentional time to get alone with God and link arms meaningfully with others. You, like many, may have questions about your calling and purpose. Or perhaps you need rest and encouragement. Wherever you are in your journey, you won't be alone at Exhale Women. Every Exhale resource and gathering is created to help you grow in relationship to God and in wisdom to help you live the life He intended you to live. I would love to connect with you at exhalewomen.org.

You are loved and God is able.

Holly

EXHALEWOMEN.ORG